# Flyer

# Flyer

The Quest to Win the
Round the World Race

*Cornelis van Rietschoten*
*Barry Pickthall*

STANFORD MARITIME   LONDON

Stanford Maritime Limited
Member Company of the George Philip Group
12 Long Acre   London WC2E 9LP
Editor Phoebe Mason

First published in Great Britain 1979
ISBN 0 540 07184 6


Designed by Bruce Thomas
Set in 11 on 13 pt Monophoto Imprint 101
and printed in Great Britain by
BAS Printers Limited, Over Wallop, Hampshire

British Library Cataloguing in Publication Data
Rietschoten, Cornelis van
    'Flyer', the quest to win the Round the World Race.
    1. Whitbread Round the World Race    2. Flyer *(Ship)*
    I. Title        II. Pickthall, Barry
    797.1'4        GV832
    ISBN 0–540–07184–6

Drawings by: Robert Das, Peter A. G. Milne
Photographs by: David Baker, Beken of Cowes, Pieter van den
Broecke, *Cape Times*, Patrice Carpentier, Gerard Dijkstra jr., Bert
Dykema, Jonathan Eastland, Colin Forbes, Adrian Ford, Jenny
Green, Billy Johnson, Aedgard Koekebakker, Pim Korver, Tom
Kroeze, Marcel Laurin, Tom Leutwyler, Adrian Morgan, Chris
Moselen, *New Zealand Herald*, David Pardon, Barry Pickthall,
Cornelis van Rietschoten, Ari Steinberg, Kees Stuip jr.,
Whitbread & Co. Ltd, Rod White, Hugh Wilson

# Contents

𝔹

Soestdijk Palace, March 1979

Since the beginning, I have been able to follow the construction of the "Flyer".

I have also been kept informed about the scrupulous preparations for this great race, preparations based on expert knowledge and great dedication.

The successful termination of such a journey around the world is only possible if one has a team in which everyone works together wholeheartedly in order to achieve the desired goal.

It is the great achievement of Conny van Rietschoten that he has been able to inspire a crew of enthusiastic men who came from so many places on our globe, in such a way that a result like this victory in such an extremely difficult race became possible.

I am very glad to see that there still are men who are willing to fight the seas with courage and perseverance.

It is an excellent idea to write down all the details of this enthralling race and to give us all the chance to follow the adventures of the "Flyer".

The Prince of the Netherlands

In the fifty-odd years which I have been able to divide between the sport of sailing and the business of helping to produce boats, there has been an opportunity to become acquainted with many extremely competent people from whom much could be learned.

In the field of boat production one learns at an early age that the success or failure of a particular project is very largely a matter of those who handle the boat and direct the sailing operation.

Among successful projects, there are two which are outstanding in my mind, not only because each was an important success but more because of the similar way in which both persons demonstrated the importance of a well rounded and balanced approach to the target.

In each case, the fact that a relatively large boat was involved dictated very careful and thorough long-range planning. This has to start with the first discussion of fundamental design, then continue through a long period where innumerable details must be worked out with the builder. In this stage the builder has great opportunity to contribute to the success of the project.

Simultaneously, very vital decisions are required relating to sails, which furnish the all-important driving power.

Then comes crew selection and the ability to get the most out of the crew, including the essential matter of training and, perhaps more important, execution of the competitive sailing.

Once launched there is the obvious but too often neglected importance of getting out under sail just as much as possible, sailing as often and as far as the schedule permits, and then last but by no means least, the ability to handle both boat and crew under often demanding conditions and over a long period of time.

It was my great good fortune to work with, and learn from, Harold

Vanderbilt in 1936 and 1937 with *Ranger*'s America's Cup defense and then to have an experience fundamentally parallel in the production of *Flyer*.

Right from the moment her skipper came into our office in the early summer of '75, and through many design sessions as well as building discussions and equipment selection, on through launching and first trials and later the specific preparation for the big race, and right through to the finish at Portsmouth, her skipper demonstrated a skill and drive that deservedly brings the title of 'The Flying Dutchman' to Cornelis van Rietschoten.

Sincerely,

Roderick Stephens, Jr.

This story is dedicated to the crew of *Flyer*. Their effort, team spirit and good companionship made this whole exercise both possible and worthwhile. I am only sorry that Adrian Ford is not with us any more to share this memory.

Cornelis van Rietschoten

# Return

They were out in the streets of Rotterdam in thousands, honking horns, blowing trumpets, waving flags and chanting. They came in cars, lorries, buses and on foot to stand six deep along the waterfront; the old and young, the middle-aged and even bewildered toddlers. They were all there to join in on one of the biggest, noisiest receptions ever seen on the banks of the Waterweg – to catch a glimpse and welcome home Holland's latest heroes.

It was a cold foggy morning on that day, April 4, 1978, but it seemed that the whole of Rotterdam, undaunted by the weather, had forsaken work to watch the spectacle. *Flyer*, 65 ft long, was dwarfed by the armada of shipping that had turned out to escort her up-river, and in comparison looked far too small to have braved a round the world race, let alone won it. Sails were furled and her crew returned the waves from the crowds as they motored past, while the air was filled with the noise of ships' sirens and cheers from the shore.

His Royal Highness Prince Bernhard had been the first to step aboard when the yacht berthed earlier at Hook of Holland, to congratulate her skipper, Cornelis van Rietschoten – Conny to his friends – for this spectacular triumph over fourteen other competitors in the Whitbread Round the World Race. He was joined by relatives of the crew, friends, and others closely involved with the boat for this final voyage upriver to her berth alongside the Royal Maas Yacht Club, though none could have visualized the tumultuous welcome in store for them. Amid the cheering, shouting and music, champagne flowed, corks flying high into the air, and congratulatory telegrams were read out from Queen Juliana, from the Prime Minister and many other prominent people. There were speeches, presentations and toasts. The whole of Holland seemed to want to shake these victors by the hand.

It was a dull, overcast day that matched that on which the race had started from Portsmouth back in August of the previous year. Then the heavens had opened to drench the crews and two thousand spectator craft. The starter's cannon from Southsea Castle sent the yachts off on an epic 27,000 mile voyage, stopping first at Cape Town, then Auckland and Rio de Janiero before returning through the Solent to Portsmouth. Hard-driving rain that quickly soaked through to the skin did little to dampen the enthusiasm that radiated from the competing yachts, nor the heart-felt admiration from all who watched them depart. Each had heard of, and some had already experienced, the fierce gales of the Southern Ocean, the giant breaking seas and intense cold. None were under any illusions: this was to be a hard race, the adventure of a lifetime, and a supreme test of strength and skill.

Yet one of the fiercest gales to be experienced was to be right at the finish some nine months later. Winds gusting up to force 12 were to greet *Flyer* as she surfed back into the Solent, first blowing out her 2.2 oz heavy spinnaker, then forcing the crew to cut the tack to lower the shooter as she rolled from gunwale to gunwale through high standing waves to finish some $59\frac{1}{2}$ hours ahead of her nearest rival.

Prince Bernhard joining *Flyer* at the Hook of Holland and meeting Conny's wife Inger.

Coming up the Waterweg to Rotterdam.

The escort of 154 vessels.

Arriving at the Royal Maas
Yacht Club

Mr Brandenburg, Harbour Master of Rotterdam, presents the skipper with a special cup commemorating this eventful day.

Prince Bernhard and Inger
van Rietschoten enjoy the
proceedings at the Royal Maas
Yacht Club.

# Early History

Van Rietschoten is an old established seafaring name. Many of Conny's forefathers had been captains of those great ships that plied their trade to the New World and the Far East around the treacherous Capes of Good Hope and the Horn. It was only the pleading of his great grandmother – herself brought up in the world of clipper ships – that finally brought the family ashore. She persuaded her husband to join a partnership fitting out sailing ships in Rotterdam rather than continue sailing them on the high seas. Though the partnership was dissolved some little while later, the company headed by Jan Jacob van Rietschoten soon flourished, fitting out many of the great ships that maintained the Dutch before the First World War as one of the leading maritime trading nations.

Born in 1926, Cornelis van Rietschoten was brought up in this nautical environment and inherited much of his drive and dedication from his father and grandfather. He has tasted most sides of life. Though brought up with the comfort of a secure family background, the war years left him almost starving ad destitute, and before reaching the boardroom of one of Holland's largest electrical combines he worked on the shop floor making machine tools in factories in England and Denmark while studying engineering at night school. He is also a man with a strong competitive spirit, determined not merely to succeed but to be outstanding in everything he tackles. He freely admits that he is at his best when pitting his skills against the elements rather than other men, and had he not been introduced to sailing at such an early age would have undoubtedly taken up a sport such as mountaineering. Not only is he a good shot, having enjoyed hunting trophies in Africa, Alaska and in the Austrian mountains, where he has a shooting lodge, but a golfer of some repute who played to a single-figure handicap.

Conny's first taste of salt spray came at the tender age of three aboard his father's Twelve Metre *Copeja*, a yacht that won a horde of first prizes. He and his two elder brothers learned to sail in a 12 ft Jol class clinker dinghy with a balanced lug rig, a type of boat that can still be seen sailing in Holland. It was an ideal trainer, and stored aboard the family's next yacht,

Conny as a three year old aboard his father's Twelve Metre yacht *Copeja* on a day's sail with family and friends.

The sleek gaff-rigged *Copeja*, one of the fastest Twelve Metres in Holland at the time.

The Royal Maas Yacht Club at Rotterdam organized many day races in the 1930s. A view of the fleet from *Copeja*.

the ketch *Maybe*, it was lowered over the side for the children to sail whenever she was anchored. In the early days the van Rietschoten family sailed together every weekend, and summer vacations were always spent either sailing in the Baltic or crossing the North Sea for Cowes Week to watch those great J Class yachts racing in the Solent. By now the family business in Rotterdam was thriving, fitting out not sailing ships but the early steamships and liners, so grandfather van Rietschoten, also called Jan Jacob, decided to design a new yacht with the aim of fulfilling a lasting ambition to sail round the world. He and Cornelis's father designed his dream ship, which was eventually named *Maybe* because during her construction the word was often used, e.g. 'Maybe we should . . .'. Unfortunately, though, she was launched too late for grandfather to fulfil his ambition. Then in his seventies, he found that all his sailing friends had either passed on or become too old to join him on this world cruise, and he himself died soon afterwards, just before the Second World War.

During the war years the van Rietschotens, like so many other Dutch families, suffered badly under the German Occupation. Cornelis himself was only thirteen at the outbreak of war and so escaped the early roundup of youngsters sent to the Fatherland. Cornelis's eldest brother, Jan Jacob, who carried the family name for the firstborn, was eighteen at the time of the Occupation but managed to escape with a friend, evading the German patrols one night to paddle across the North Sea in a canoe. This dangerous voyage was completed in seventy-eight hours and gave them the chance to join the Dutch Section of the Special Operations Executive (SOE) based in England. Later, Jan Jacob parachuted back into Holland to work with the Resistance movement, but was caught up in the England Spiel, one of the major blunders during the war, quickly captured and imprisoned.

The Germans managed to capture one of the first agents to be dropped, and after interrogation forced him to broadcast a message back to England saying that they had all landed safely and that the next men could follow. The authorities had in fact foreseen this possibility and had trained the Resistance parachutists to include a special coded message should they ever be caught. Unfortunately for Jan Jacob and the many others with him, those same authorities then chose to ignore the secret warning and dropped further men right into the arms of waiting German patrols. Later, he was one of the few to escape, but fell into the hands of a Dutch collaborator while trying to make contact with the Underground movement, was handed back to the Germans and executed in 1944.

Joan Peter, two years senior to Cornelis, was another of the van Rietschoten brothers to die during the War. He worked as mate on a Rhine cargo barge to escape the deportation of young Dutchmen to Germany for forced labour. Unfortunately the barge was in Duisburg during the first Allied thousand-bomber raid, and as searchlights lit the skies to pinpoint the planes as they droned overhead, a stick of bombs dropped right by them. The skipper was blown overboard; though badly wounded in the blast himself, Joan Peter dived in after him but didn't survive the ordeal.

The school Cornelis attended was taken over by the Germans, and studies were continued at home with a teacher coming round for an hour each week to check that he had done his homework. Final exams were forgotten for fear that the Occupation forces might pick the children up and send them to Germany, and Cornelis remained a prisoner in the family home, hidden at times in a secret room built into the eaves of the roof. The entrance to this prison was through a cleverly disguised wardrobe, and the secret door, faced with concrete on the reverse side so that it would not give a hollow sound when tapped, was opened by turning a coathook at the back of the cupboard. Cornelis made use of this cubbyhole whenever German patrols were sighted, and once inside would lock the handle with a wooden arm that swung up to jam the mechanism in place.

As the War progressed it became increasingly difficult for the young people hiding from the Germans, and Cornelis eventually decided to try to follow his eldest brother across to England. His parents did not agree at first, but eventually it was decided that he should leave Rotterdam and try to get south of the river. He and a friend got as far as the island of Dordrecht, but their timing could not have been worse. No sooner had they arrived on the island than it was suddenly occupied by a large

*Maybe* was designed for round
the world cruising but built
too late in his life for Conny's
grandfather to fulfil that
ambition.

contingent of German troops forming a defence line against a possible invasion by the Allies. It was impossible for them to escape, and for the remaining six months of the War Cornelis was forced to hide in toilets, cellars and other unsavoury places, eating what meagre rations could be spared by the local population.

Although most private yachts in Holland were stolen by the Germans during the Occupation and sailed away to the Baltic, *Maybe* was saved from being requisitioned. By good fortune she had been laid up in a canal and left stranded throughout the War when water levels were dropped by more than one metre. It took some while after peace was declared for the other yachts to be traced, but many were eventually found at Svenborg on the island of Fünen, and once *Maybe* had been recommissioned Cornelis and his father set off with some of the other owners to bring their yachts back to Holland. It was on the return voyage, and while stormbound in Cuxhaven, that they met up with a young man named Morin Scott who was taking a German yacht back to England, and a lasting friendship was formed.

Cornelis later moved to England, working in a machine tool factory at Halifax by day and studying engineering at a technical school by night. It was hard work, but he realized that he had a great deal of schooling to catch up on.

After a sailing holiday to the Azores and back aboard *Maybe* Conny returned to his work and studies in England and survived one of the worst railways crashes in Britain's history. The accident, at Peterborough, saw more than fifty people killed and a further seventy injured. Cornelis himself, riding in the next to last carriage, managed to get out and after a short stay in hospital recovered completely. 'I was very very lucky indeed,' he recalled later.

When Cornelis and Morin Scott next met it was at a London railway station. Scotty had scraped up every shilling he could find to buy a Dragon keelboat and he couldn't wait to share the news with his friend. Immediately they were planning where to take her, and in the spring of 1947 arranged to sail *Gerda* from McGruer's boatyard in Scotland down to the South Coast of England. It was an eventful voyage, south to Dartmouth via Dublin, Milford Haven and Falmouth; at one point the yacht was almost run aground as they fought against the strong currents that run between islands off the Welsh coast. However, the trip gave both Morin and Conny an insatiable taste for long-distance sailing.

Months later, after the Dragon had been sailed to Newhaven, her new home port, the two met again and Conny, having won £200 on the football pools, offered to share *Gerda*'s upkeep costs through the following year.

They next met at the Dragon Class dinner, to learn that the International Gold Cup Races, the annual Dragon World Championship, were to be held in Norway the following year. It was just the sort of trip they had been thinking about and immediately they started to lay plans to sail *Gerda* across. It was an incredible voyage for such a small yacht, and she suffered gales the whole way across the North Sea.

*Morin now takes up the story.*

Soon after leaving Harwich strong winds built up the first day out and several times the Dragon heeled over at an alarming angle as she ploughed through the seas at seven knots. Eventually the mainsail had to be lowered completely, but even then the boat continued at five knots or more under jib alone.

Both wind and seas increased throughout the night and by four o'clock in the morning the weather was at its worst. *Gerda* was pooped several times, but even without this water still came aboard as the yacht surfed down the crest of the waves. The Dragon, being so narrow, buried in the crests at the top of each wave with the result that they rose up to engulf the cabin and cockpit. At times Cornelis, whose job was to man the Vortex pump in the cabin, saw green water through the portholes on both sides of the cabin at the same time. Much later, when we had arrived in Cuxhaven, someone was to ask if there were any moments when we were scared. Conny, whose English was not very good at the time, was the first to answer. 'I sit in zee cabin, zee pump between my knees, and I looked up on one side and zee green vater through the scuttles. Den I look round at zee udder two scuttles and I zee green vater dere also. Den I look down and zee vater in zee bilge is above my knees. Den I vas frightened!'

I remained at the helm for more than nineteen hours and by four in the morning was near exhaustion. Conny was not much better, having been pumping hard, charting the course and passing up food. It was while we were at this low ebb that we were suddenly taken by surprise by a huge wave that rolled up from astern to climb right over the deck. *Gerda*'s stern was flung round and the boat thrown over onto her side, then held down by the pressure of the wind for what seemed an eternity. Water poured below filling the small yacht to six inches above the bunks and she came very close to sinking.

By ten o'clock there was still no sight of land or the shipping lane, and as the wind had veered to the southwest, I altered course towards the southeast, luffing up when I could then bearing away each time another huge waved rolled by. We had hoped to strike the coast at Terschelling and run through the West Gat into the Borndiep Channel where we could anchor, have a meal and get some sleep.

By 1130 ships were spotted on the horizon so we knew that *Gerda* was approaching the swept channel, and an hour later a buoy was sighted. Unfortunately it was ET14, ten miles to the east and downwind of West

Gat, to leave us badly off course. The idea of beating back to an open anchorage no longer had the same appeal, so instead we decided to push on for Cuxhaven. This meant another night at sea, so having been at the tiller for twenty-eight hours, I decided to change places with my friend below. I also wanted some hot food, and since Conny had not been able to light the Primus this had to be stripped down to see what the trouble was.

It took an hour and a minor fire in the cabin before the Primus was working satisfactorily, but everything below was so wet by then that nothing except methylated spirits and matches would burn. After what seemed hours, steam started to rise from the saucepan and without waiting for the soup to boil, it was poured into two mugs and gulped down. By that time *Gerda* was sailing past Huibert Gat buoy, a turning-point in the swept

Crossing the North Sea. This drawing of the Dragon *Gerda* by Colin Grierson captures the conditions that they met during much of the voyage to Norway.

channel, and we gybed across onto the new course. I was now completely exhausted, and after swapping places with Conny, fell asleep in the corner of the cabin, while *Gerda* swept on at six knots under jib.

Two hours later, though, I woke and poked my nose up through the hatch to ask how things were. 'I don't know', was Conny's reply. 'Don't know – what on earth do you mean?' I retorted, short-tempered through lack of sleep. Conny then explained that he too had just woken up from a peculiar trance. He thought the correct course had been steered somehow or other but had experienced some queer hallucinations; he was convinced that I was ashore buying methylated spirits and that the compass had taken the form of a plate of bacon and eggs on a well-laid table with knife and fork on either side!

Other vessels in sight meant they were still in the swept channel and soon afterwards JE18 buoy was picked up. I then took over the helm while Conny went below to produce a meal of scrambled eggs and bacon served in a mug and accompanied with bread, butter and steaming hot cocoa. Although the wind had eased slightly, we were so tired out that I decided that it was better not to hoist the mainsail but continue under jib alone. It was a wise decision, for by 2100 thunder clouds had rolled over once more – the prelude to yet another storm.

Between then and midnight the conditions were at their worst. The wind backed to the south and blew like blazes. Rain came down in sheets, and driven by the wind it was like needles pricking the skin, magnified a hundred times. *Gerda* tore eastwards through the pitch-black night, and they caught a last glimpse of a swept-channel buoy at around 2200. Some time around midnight the weather improved, but our knowledge of events between then and two o'clock was almost nil. Sleep overcame Conny in the cabin while I dozed at the tiller. Fortunately both wind and sea had decreased slightly after the thunder had passed over, and still under her storm rig *Gerda* could come to little harm.

At 0200 I was suddenly jerked awake, realizing that we had not seen a buoy for some considerable time. I shouted to wake Conny but there was no reply, then banged on the deck, but there was still no response. I tried to move but found that I was entirely numb from the waist down. Panic gripped me as thoughts flashed through my mind. Was I paralysed? . . . Conny was overboard . . . or paralysed too. I just didn't know, but screamed and banged on the deck like a man fighting for life. After an age Conny answered, eventually woken from a very deep sleep. By this time I was in agony, my legs and thighs filled with the pains of acute pins and needles, so Conny pulled himself together and took the tiller while I massaged my legs to bring back the circulation.

Neither one had any idea where we were. We could not remember what buoys had been passed, or the log readings. The last two hours were just a blank. The only point we could remember was a buoy flashing at six-second intervals. This had been identified on the chart by Conny as a Fl.G., but he had misread the G for a 6, and from this mythical position a course had been set which I had not steered . . . it was all a fine mess. All I could do was guess, and came up with a southeasterly course which I hoped would take *Gerda* to the Elbe Lightvessel. The fresh winds still from the south gave little chance to recuperate. Everything was still against us. Though I thought we must have been within ten miles of Helgoland, the visibility would not clear to give us a glimpse.

To get us along on a closehauled course, the mainsail was hoisted once more but with several rolls down. *Gerda* shot off throwing heavy spray back into the cockpit, but her crew were now past caring. Both did a great deal of praying and swearing, but neither seemed to have any effect. Patience ran out and it was unbearable waiting for something to happen. Eventually, after what seemed an age but was nearer two and a half hours, two ships were sighted. One appeared to be the lightvessel we had been searching for but it took another hour to get close enough to read 'Weser' on her side. This was a disappointment, for it meant that *Gerda* was well off course, but the chart showed the outer Elbe lightship only nine miles away on a broad reach.

With the tide with us at last, we passed the Elbe 2 lightship at 0930 hours and at 1100 Elbe 3 was abeam. The wind fell lighter, but after the battering of the night before it was with great difficulty that we persuaded ourselves that the reefs could be shaken out. At 1430 *Gerda* entered Amerikahaven, $62\frac{1}{2}$ hours out from Harwich, having sailed across the North Sea at an average speed of just over five knots. The Frontier Control Service couldn't have been more helpful. In a short time we were whisked away by car to drink tea in the mess. Baths followed, and then more drinks while papers were set in order and a launch ordered to tow *Gerda* to Kiel. After that it was a long sleep. The following day the Dragon was towed through the canal to Kiel where we spent some time recuperating. Hands had suffered most during the voyage, and neither of us recovered full feeling in our fingers until we were in Arendal some three weeks later.

The less said about the racing the better, for the ageing *Gerda* was not the most competitive of Dragons. Compared with her stripped-out counterparts, she was one of the heaviest boats there, being fitted out for cruising with berths, stove and other luxuries. However, these small comforts did have some uses during the racing, for in one event the wind dropped away to nothing to leave the fleet drifting astern on the tide. *Gerda* was the only competitor to carry a heavy anchor and sufficient cable to cope with the 700

*Maze* crashing through the Solent soon after the start of the Fastnet Race in 1957, in which she was dismasted.

ft depth of water. Their kedge held her firmly, and they spent the rest of the afternoon cooking and eating a fresh salmon while watching the fleet go by stern first. There were more than sixty starters in the race, so they had a lot to watch as their position improved from last to first, but just when they thought they had a chance of winning, the race was cancelled. It was the nearest that *Gerda* ever got to the winners' rostrum, but at least the salmon was tasty.

Although the pair earned neither cup nor prize during the regatta, Crown Prince Olaf called them to stand up at the prizegiving, proclaiming them the best sailors of the regatta – a tribute worth more than any prizes.

After this interlude Cornelis started to work at the family business in Rotterdam. Because his father was very much in charge, Cornelis was given the opportunity to start his own business in the pharmaceutical trade. His father suffered from withered muscles in one arm which at the time medical science could not cure, until he met up with a little known scientist whose enzyme injections were claimed to cure almost all ills. They certainly worked, and so impressed was he with his miracle cure that he financed the scientist to further his research. Cornelis then set up a company to market the injections and if possible recover his father's investment. In fact, he made a great success of it which repaid the initial expenditure many times over.

During this time he continued sailing, first crewing aboard a well known pre-war boat, *Olivier van Noort*, owned by another Dutchman, Albert Goudriaan, and later had a half share in an Robert Clark designed yawl called *Maze*. His partner was an old school friend, Aad van Stolk, who had built the boat and then asked Cornelis to join him. They competed in several Cowes Weeks and Fastnet Races, and once took a third place in the Santander Race.

Conny learned a great deal from this boat, although she was very different from modern racers like *Flyer*. *Maze* had just one spinnaker aboard compared to the ten carried on the Round the World Race, and one synthetic-fibre sail, for the rest were made of cotton sailcloth.

It was during the 1957 Fastnet that *Maze* was dismasted in gale conditions while rounding Portland Bill. 'It was a scary moment, I can tell you,' Conny told me when recounting the event. They were close enough to the shore for people there to realize the trouble they were in and someone raised the alarm to call the Lifeboat out from Weymouth. Unfortunately her crew steered straight for the strong tidal race that flows round this stark headland, having been told that *Maze* had been caught up in the stream. In fact they had been disabled further out from the race and made it back into harbour under jury rig.

Two years after this, sailing was brought to an abrupt halt when Cornelis contracted tuberculosis, forcing him to spend a year slowly recovering in a Swiss sanatorium. It looked as though it would be the end of his sailing career, for there are few doctors who recommend a cold and wet atmosphere for post-convalescence.

Having recovered, Cornelis handed the pharmacetical business back to the scientist and at the age of thirty-two took over control of the family business interests in Rotterdam. It was a demanding position which left little time to spare for sailing.

# Decisions

It was some thirteen years before the sea bug bit once more. By this time the family business had been sold and Cornelis had retired from a daily office routine, and at the age of forty-five he was keen to find fresh interests. It was newspaper reports of the original Whitbread Round the World Race in 1973–4 that first suggested a circumnavigation. His grandfather had designed and built *Maybe* specifically for this adventure, but left it too late in life to achieve the ambition. Cornelis on the other hand was young enough to take on the challenge, and the fact that a second Whitbread Race was planned lent more appeal to the idea, for a race would satisfy his competitive spirit as well as a sense of adventure. His enquiry was one of the first to be recieved by Whitbreads in London, although at the time he was by no means sure that he was sufficiently fit or experienced to cope with the challenge. Thirteen years away from the sea was a long time, and the technical changes in ocean racing had been enormous.

After drawing up a list of pros and cons, his confidence was given little encouragement when he found that the minus column heavily outweighed any positive points he could muster towards entering the race. However, never one to give up easily, the problems were churned over and over in his mind until answers were found and gradually the list took on a brighter aspect. Initially, the positive points were just four: 'I've been sailing all my life, have a strong competitive spirit, have been trained to manage people and projects, and can get good people to do the jobs that I am unsure about.'

By far the biggest hurdle was coming to terms with the many technical changes since his sailing days on *Maze*. Rigs, for instance, were now much more sophisticated. Apart from the change from wood to metal spars there was now much greater emphasis towards control of mast rake and bend while sailing. The running backstays on *Maze* were taken to Highfield levers on either quarter and always locked in one position when sailing to windward. Today backstays and many other elements of the rigging are adjusted continually to suit the conditions and play an important part in optimizing sail shape and trim. There are now so many different sail sizes, shapes and constructions available (and heavily promoted) that it is hard to choose which combinations are better for various conditions of wind strength, angle and sea. In earlier days reefing the main was a major event, taking perhaps ten or fifteen minutes, but now it is a simple two-minute operation and thus liable to be done and undone more frequently. *Maze* had one spinnaker whereas *Flyer* had nine different types and carried them in a much greater range of wind strengths and angles. Early mainsails were controlled with the sheet, but on *Flyer* the sail was trimmed in six or seven different ways.

Another problem was crew. 'My friends were obviously not the ones to have on board', he confided later. 'Apart from being my age, they would have wanted to weigh the boat down with a great deal more comforts than the present generation of hot-shot sailors, who take a much more professional attitude towards racing. My worry was whether I could cope with these much younger lads who have a completely different outlook on life.'

In June 1975 he visited the Sparkman & Stephens design office in New York to discuss the project with Olin and Rod Stephens. Cornelis had long been impressed by the firm's talent for combining strong, seaworthy and fast characteristics into their yacht designs, exemplified by *Sayula*, a previous S&S production design that had won the first Whitbread Round the World Race. After talking over the project for an hour, however, Olin, a quiet and polite introvert by nature, could not help but voice his concern for this potential client who had not set foot on a racing yacht for so many years. However painful, he felt the question had to be asked, and with eyes averted and voice filled with embarrassed undertones, said, 'Can you really handle this – you honestly think you can do a race like this?' The answer was short and positive, and later Cornelis was to produce such a detailed plan of campaign that from then onwards there were to be no further reservations about his ability – in fact, the pair have got on famously ever since.

The final decision to enter the race was made during a short holiday in Germany during August of 1975. It was here in a small hotel that he had time to finalize plans and determine in his own mind how the campaign would be managed.

# Foundations for Success

The first consideration was to complete the course without serious damage or loss of life. This concern for safety and reliability took precedence over winning and shows up continually throughout the preparation for the race. Whenever an idea improved speed but reduced reliability another solution had to be found. Cornelis always felt that the ingredients for overall honours were good navigation, seamanship, sail handling – and luck. 'There's always a great deal of luck required for this kind of racing', he said at the prizegiving.

However, careful planning is also equally important, and eventually it was Conny's meticulous preparation that gave him the edge over his rivals. He freely admits that early in life he was greatly influenced by Paavo Nurmi, the famous Finnish long-distance runner who won three Olympic Gold Medals before the war. Nurmi would race with a stopwatch in his hand, then on the last leg throw away the watch and sprint for the finish. He left nothing to chance, and it was this fastidious approach that Conny followed.

The yacht was to be run like a business would be, using normal management practices. The skipper, naturally, took ultimate responsibility with watch leaders acting as middle management and individual jobs on board delegated according to experience or qualifications. Specific job descriptions were drawn up for key crewmen (see Appendix) and checked over by Rod Stephens, a very experienced ocean racer in his own right and partner in the design firm, who added a few pointers of his own. In practice this cut out a great deal of petty argument, for there could never be any dispute over jobs. A number of photocopies were run off, so that if any were lost there was always another available. Telling someone to get out his list of duties and read it was very effective and didn't need to be repeated.

The problem of compatibility was anticipated in part by banning politics and complaints about the food as topics of conversation on board. This did cut out many arguments, clashes of personality and tense atmospheres that inevitably occur between crew members drawn from all walks of life, living in cramped and unvarying conditions for extended periods. They could talk about sex (and frequently did), good food, sport – indeed, anything but politics. The extensive pre-race trials and passages were intended to show up crew problems as much as to refine the boat, and to build up a team that would continue to work effectively together.

Compared with some light displacement racing boats launched at the time, the drawings for *Flyer* were far from extreme. Her lines, with moderate displacement (24.6 tons) and of fin and skeg underwater profile, are probably best described as being a modern replacement for the S&S design for the Swan 65 built by Nautor in Finland. Though only eight inches longer overall, *Flyer*'s waterline, which dictates theoretical maximum speed, is some 2 ft 9 in longer than that of the Swan. Beam measurements are identical, but draft was a fraction deeper on the later design, and *Flyer*'s displacement is a ton lighter to improve light air performance. From the results of the first Whitbread Round the World Race (WRTWR), it was decided that a yacht of similar size to *Sayula* would stand the best chance of winning the overall handicap prize. Anything much smaller could prove an uncomfortable proposition in the Southern Ocean, and be crowded and weighed down by the necessary amounts of stores, spares, safety and personal gear, etc. Larger yachts have been shown to be difficult to sail up to their rated handicaps.

The Whitbread Races are handicap events designed to equalize the chances of winning for all those taking part, though there are overall and leg prizes for elapsed-time winners. All yachts have to be measured to a complicated international rule (IOR) to give a measured length which is normally very close to the actual waterline length. Utilising valuable experience from the first RTWR and their analysis of the weather and current patterns along the route, the Race Committee estimated the length in miles of each leg, then applied a time on distance formula to calculate final handicap times. Displacement hulls have a theoretical maximum speed related to their waterline length, and usually predicted as $1.4 \times \sqrt{LWL}$ (feet). This formula gives *Flyer* (49 ft 9 in LWL) a top speed on paper of 9.87 knots, while *Traité de Rome*, a much smaller yacht with a waterline of 35 ft 1 in, has a speed of 8.29 knots. In fact boats often exceed these theoretical hull speeds in surfing conditions, when they are thrust forward and plane down wave faces. *Flyer* often exceeded 16 knots for short bursts during the heavy weather experienced in the Southern Oceans, but *average* speeds rarely climbed above this figure.

Aluminium was chosen as the construction material for the simple reason that it offers a 30% weight advantage over fibreglass. Wood was never considered, for one point that Cornelis remembered all too well from his earlier racing days was the amount of maintenance required, and the problem of leaks. Building quotes were received from five yards, four of

Months of careful planning went into *Flyer*'s design before any construction started. One of the special features of the deck layout was the separate cockpit for sail trimmers, constructed around the mainmast and protected by a wide coaming where halyard and auxiliary winches were eventually mounted. Aft of that and on either side of the companionway opening are the compartments for gas bottles, each holding six bottles of propane for cooking. The high toerail visible at the bow was continued around the deck to give security.

Working in the engine room, designed to ensure that all the machinery was accessible and easy to service.

A second set of instruments used by the sail trimmers in the forward cockpit.

which were in America, but when prices were compared it was Wolter Huisman's company, the Overijsselse Jachtwerf in Vollenhove, Holland, that proved to be the most favourable. He accepted the job promising that *Flyer* would be ready to sail away on the first Saturday in April 1977. The yacht had to be ready on time, for Cornelis had already pencilled in a complete training and race programme as a buildup to the Round the World Race. This included extensive trials in Holland, a training cruise across to America, and participation in the Transatlantic Race back, prior to returning to Huisman for final modifications. Between launching in April and the start off Portsmouth in late August, *Flyer* and most of her crew had sailed 10,000 miles together.

Cornelis sought as much advice as possible at the start of the project from the experts he knew, to pool current knowledge on rigs, sails, deck

Cabins were totally enclosed,
not just to afford privacy and
quiet for the crew off watch
but to keep those areas as dry
as possible – a real advantage
in cold weather. The wide
passageway running between
saloon and forepeak made it
possible to fold even the
biggest sails below decks.

equipment and design, as well as a dietitian's advice on food and menus. He talked to Tjerk Romke de Vries, the Dutchman who had crewed aboard *Sayula* on the first race, to ask what improvements he would make to the Swan deck layout. The most important point he made was that there should be a separate cockpit for sail trimmers, protected by a wrap-around coaming where halyard and ancillary winches could be mounted, and also suggested that a deeper stern cockpit would protect the crew better. Both ideas were drawn into *Flyer*'s design. During the modification period prior to the race itself, there was one loud dissenting voice wanting to do away with the centre cockpit. Indeed, this particular crew wanted to remove most of the ideas that had been built into the boat, and in the end he left. Among other criticisms, he felt that the crew would be forever falling into the cockpit, and in a way he had the last laugh: it was Conny himself who was the only one to trip up, and cut his leg badly, the wound taking three months to heal. By the end of the race, however, the crew were in agreement that this was one of the better ideas on the boat, for it gave excellent protection to people tending sails.

Another point that Cornelis specified was that the yacht should be as watertight as possible, with the layout below drawn up with crew comfort in mind. Crew cabins were totally closed, not just to afford some degree of privacy and quiet for those off watch, but to keep them as dry as possible. This partitioning added considerable weight and would be unacceptable in an ordinary offshore racer, but the philosophy of dry berths and good food

The eating area, just big enough for one watch at a time and next to the passageway. There was a gimballed rack over the table to hold drinks and condiments.

went a long way towards keeping morale high during the extended periods at sea.

Cornelis also insisted that *Flyer* should be designed with a separate engine compartment, with the machinery raised as high as possible to reduce the chance of breakdowns through flooding. He had always thought that the separate compartment built into *Maybe* had been a good principle, for it allowed plenty of space around the engine so that all parts were readily accessible and simple to service. The engine is in fact one of the most important pieces of ancillary equipment aboard a long-distance ocean racer, for it has to be run at least four hours each day to charge batteries, and in this case to keep the deepfreeze in operation. Without this 'iron topsail' batteries quickly run down, to leave the boat without power for the radio, sailing instruments and lighting. A good deepfreeze can be left without power for twenty-four hours, but after that food starts to thaw and must be thrown away. (Engine propulsion was not mandatory, however, and installation details were not specified.) The unit chosen was a Volvo diesel MD32A. Lack of space meant that one side of the engine compartment had to be left completely open to the companionway linking the saloon and stern cabins, making it a noisy installation. However, one benefit was that while running the engine heated the boat and offered an efficient drying area for wet clothing.

Hugh Wilson

Adrian Ford

The first crew member to be enrolled was Hugh Wilson, an English shipwright from Swanage in Dorset, who had sailed with one of Conny's sons out to the Caribbean the year before, acting as navigator on the return voyage. It was this broad experience that Cornelis was looking for, and it was arranged that Hugh would work with Huisman from September 1976 throughout the building. He's a short stocky fellow who had already packed a wealth of experience into his 25 years, has a great sense of humour, and more often than not is seen with a cigar between the fingers of one hand and a beer mug raised in the other. He was invaluable on board, for not only was he a good sailor but knew the ship like the back of his hand and was able to solve most problems during the race almost before they arose.

Another decision to be made at the start of the project concerned sails. The advantage of working with just one sailmaker with world-wide links was obvious enough, but Conny required much more than this. A slick sales letter from the Hood sail loft in the United States, who had heard through the grapevine that he was preparing for the race, coincided with an approach he was about to make to them. Hoods had already been well recommended, but Cornelis wanted much more than just the best sails: he also needed two experienced sailmakers involved in the project from the outset, who would join up with the crew for the Transatlantic and Whitbread Races. It was a deal that appealed to Hood, and eventually two New Zealanders, one from the Marblehead loft, took leave from their jobs to take on the *Flyer* colours.

Simon Willis, the more experienced sailor and someone for whom sails were an obsession, acted as watch leader on the Transatlantic Race, and though a hard task master at times, demanding constant sail changes, taught the crew a great deal about sail handling and trimming. Adrian Ford, his number two, played the part of sailmaker, repairing the sails on a sewing machine set up in the saloon. Simon left the crew before the start of the Round the World Race to take up the managership of the Hood service loft in Auckland, where he was to be on hand to repair *Flyer*'s wardrobe in readiness for the stormy third leg to Rio.

Adrian, on the other hand, not only worked on the pre-launch preparation and trials but remained with *Flyer* throughout and did a great job keeping the sails in one piece, often under the most trying conditions. On deck he acted as sheet tailer to the starboard watch, but during heavy weather and for some considerable time afterwards he was normally found below, running up torn sails on the sewing machine, or rebuilding spinnakers that had blown out. At each port of call he would take the complete wardrobe to the nearest sail loft to check each sail individually and oversee their servicing. His one fault was that he smoked too much –

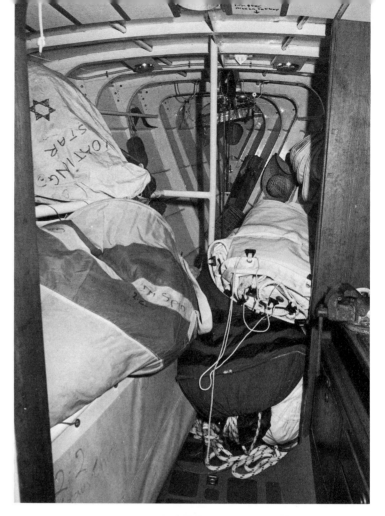

All sails were stowed in bins
forward, which doubled as
pipe cots for some of the crew
in port.

normally forty or fifty a day – but his delicious curry dinners served up whenever the resident cook wanted a night off more than made up for his overindulgence with the weed.

Sadly, Adrian and a friend were lost at sea during a passage from Gibraltar to Poole the following winter. No one knows exactly what happened: *Scorpio*, a 35 ft racing yacht he was delivering back to her home port, was found lying on a beach ten miles south of Vigo on the northwest coast of Spain with her dinghy alongside. It is thought likely that the yacht was running for shelter from the storm that had raged during the previous few days, and that Adrian and his crew were swept overboard.

A ketch rig was chosen to give a wide variety of sail combinations and in order that no sails would be too large for one watch to handle on their own. She was drawn with a larger mizzen than those on the ketch-rigged Swan 65s, to improve reaching and downwind performance. *Flyer* showed her best speeds when close-reaching, and on all points of sailing in strong winds. The only time *Flyer* gave away speed to the sloop-rigged Swan 65 *Kings Legend* was in light airs, either sailing closehauled or going dead downwind, where she proved to be undercanvased.

Thirty-five sails were supplied at the start of the Round the World Race with a further six ordered during the race to replace those that were blown out, deemed unrepairable, or had lost their shape. The storm sails required by the rules were never used and remained packed in their sail bin. The fleet as a whole had to fight against very few bad gales, in contrast to the anticipated conditions, and the furthest *Flyer* ever reduced sail was to a cutter rig for twenty-four hours soon after leaving New Zealand. Two small jibs were hoisted, one on the inner forestay, which allowed headsail area to be reduced quickly if conditions suddenly deteriorated.

For the first and last legs of the race, a Hood Gemini twin luff groove headsail foil system was fitted over the jibstay to speed up and simplify the many light weather sail changes expected. For the second and third legs they switched back to hanked-on headsails on a bare rod stay because there was some doubt about whether the special luff tape on the sails set in the Gemini foil would stand up to the rigours of the Southern Ocean. In practice, however, there were very few problems experienced with the headfoil system, and certainly little trouble with the luff tape tearing away from the sail. In heavy winds the friction between the two sails in a peel change made it worth dropping the old sail before hoisting the new one, but the foil still saved time over piston hanks.

The sailcloth chosen had a soft finish to make packing sails below decks as easy as possible. Heavily resinated cloth may hold its shape better in strong winds, but is only suitable for short offshore racing where sails can be refolded and packed either on deck or on the dockside once the race is

The galley, with a four-burner stove, deepfreeze, fridge, double sink, and ample stowage for everyday items. It was arranged so that the cook could brace himself in position whatever the yacht's motion.

over. It would be quite impossible to fold this material below decks without ruining the finish, which is where sails have to be packed on long ocean races. Cloth seams, a common chafe point, were treated with Duroseam, a special resin applied over the stitching to protect against wear, and this worked extremely well. On the last leg, where a great deal of windward work was expected, chafe was further reduced by shrouding the stanchions, lifelines and rigging screws in pockets of sailcloth.

Food at sea was another matter that required a good deal of thought. Menus were planned for each day of a seven-day cycle of three set meals per day, to ensure that the food was not only appetising and not wasted, but offered the correct amount of calories and vitamins. Menus were made

Would it ever break? After Inger failed to crack the bottle, Conny took over
the time-honoured task of naming the yacht – but it took another two
violent close-range throws before the glass eventually shattered, soaking him
as much as *Flyer*.

around three basic ingredients, deep-frozen meat, freeze-dried food and Jack Mie bread, and augmented by fresh fruit, eggs and vegetables for the first two or three weeks of each leg. It was from an American yachting magazine that Cornelis first learned about the possible advantages of freeze-dried food and sent off for samples from a dealer in Miami. The two main advantages of dehydrated over frozen food are that it is even simpler to prepare (just add boiling water) and is very light. The packages could be stowed virtually anywhere in the ship without affecting trim, and the fresh water required to mix with it was stored in tanks directly above the keel to act as ballast. But as salt was already included, cooking with sea water made the food too salty: thus more fresh water had to be carried.

The services of Martinair, the largest air caterers in Holland, were used to help prepare the menus, and Siebe Terband, the Party Service Manager, flew across to America with Cornelis to visit Mountain House Foods, the leading manufacturers of freeze-dried food. The two spent three days munching their way through plate after plate of samples and eventually prepared a complete list of requirements. The food was given a final testing during the Transatlantic Race where it met with everyone's approval, and from then on there was a crate of Mountain House products sent to each port of call, packed as daily menus in large-size cans.

Water was pumped from main tanks into a day tank. Of the total capacity of 1400 litres about 200 would be left at the end of each leg; daily consumption for all cooking and drinking purposes came to about 40 L. The small daily-use tank made it easy to observe the rate of use. Water issued for private use was not fully used; 2 L per week per man seemed to be the average. Although many accounts of ocean passage-making describe collecting rainwater, it was found on this race that to rely to any extent on rain would have been unwise.

*Flyer* was completed a few days ahead of schedule and for this all credit should go to Wolter Huisman, who did an excellent job. She was extremely well built and never presented worrying symptoms of structural weakness, which appeared on several other boats in the race. Launching was held up by an equally strong bottle of champagne that just refused to break. Inger, Conny's wife, had a couple of tries at naming the yacht, then the skipper took over, but it was only after two violent throws at close range that the glass eventually shattered, soaking him as much as *Flyer*.

Crew selection was now the most immediate task, and during the trials in the North Sea a number of hopeful applicants were invited aboard. Aedgard Koekebakker from Breskens, the eventual rigger on board, had already been working with Hugh Wilson and Adrian Ford during the building stage. So keen was he to join *Flyer* that he resigned as managing director of a prospering Dutch firm of yacht equipment suppliers. He's an

Wolter Huisman with Rod
Stephens during *Flyer*'s trials

Sailing trials on the Ijsselmeer
with Urk in the background

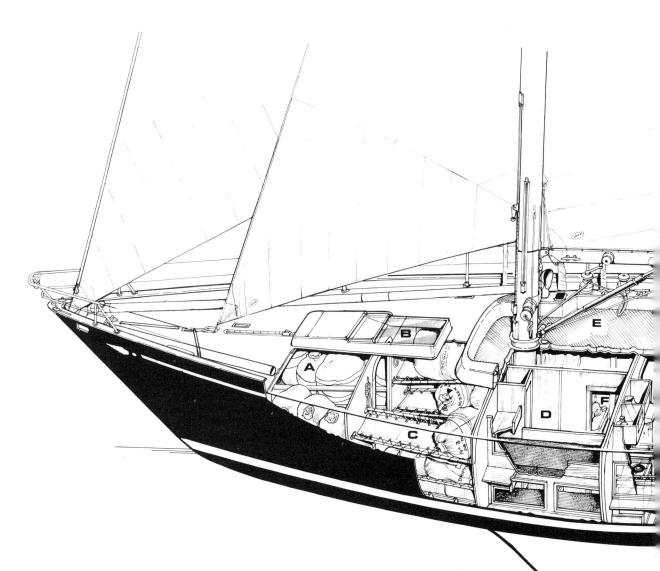

A   Sail bins for the thirty-eight sails carried during the
    race
B   Tool stowage and workbench
C   Sail bins, which double as bunks in harbour
D   Port crew cabin
E   Hydraulic boom vang
F   Sewing machine for sail repairs
G   400 litre deepfreeze in galley
H   Cockpit for sail handling
I   Drying room open to the engine room and next to the
    head
J   Chart table in radio/navigation cabin

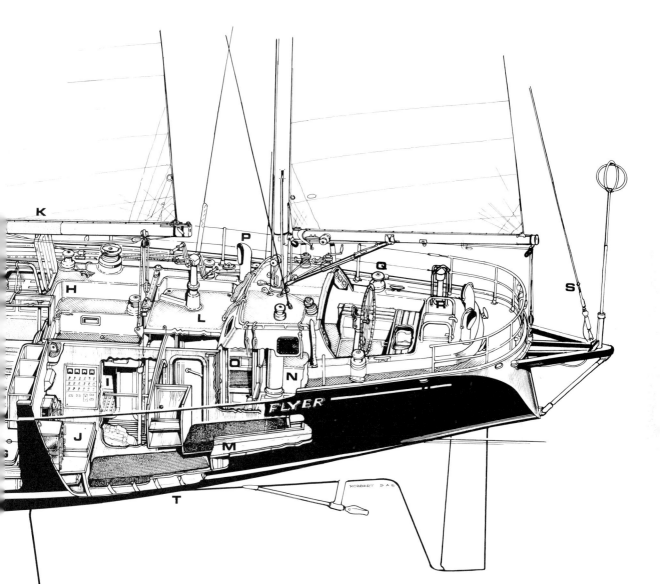

K   Main boom
L   Coffeegrinder winch on starboard side
M   Captain's bunk
N   Interior of doghouse
O   Watch captain/cook cabin
P   Ventilator on Dorade box
Q   Lewmar winch, one of the twenty-two winches on
    board
R   Webasto heater chimney
S   Mizzen backstay on bumpkin
T   Skeg

Entering the Ijsselmeer on the
way to the North Sea

Aedgard Koekebakker

Bert Dykema

extremely tough sailor with a good deal of blue-water experience behind him, having spent a term with the Dutch Navy and competed in a previous Transatlantic Race with the famous Dutch sailor Kees Bruynzeel, as well as in many top yacht racing events including the Admiral's Cup. His job on board was starboard watch leader, with special responsibility for the rig and safety equipment.

One of the early recruits was Bruce Ashwood, an ex petty officer in the Royal Navy, who had served under Morin Scott as a bosun aboard the sail training ship *Royalist*. He went on a Volvo service course to become familiar with *Flyer*'s engine and was able to keep the machinery running through thick and thin. Though the smallest among the crew, he's a tough little character and on deck became winch grinder for the port watch.

Once sailing trials were complete, *Flyer* set off on her shakedown cruise

Tied up at Marblehead inside the two American Twelve Metres *Courageous* and *Independence*.

to America, calling in at Lymington (one of Conny's favourite harbours), Palma in the Canaries, and Bermuda, finally arriving in Marblehead, Mass. on May 31, seven days ahead of schedule, to tie up next to the two Twelve Metre yachts, *Independence* and *Courageous*, being prepared for the America's Cup trials. The voyage had shown up a number of minor shortcomings, mainly chafe points where lines rubbed on sails and booms, or sails on lifelines, or which snagged on the boom. These cannot always be foreseen at the drawing board stage, and Aedgard and Simon drew up a list of changes to be made before the Transatlantic Race eighteen days away. Stainless steel halyard wire was changed for galvanized, which was generally found easier to handle and less likely to kink, or to strand and produce fish hooks; also the original Lewmar sheet and guy snap shackles and blocks were replaced by Schaeffer snatchblocks, Rondal standing blocks and Sparcraft cam-operated snap shackles.

Two days later Ted Hood and the experts from his loft took a day off from testing Twelves to sail on *Flyer* and go through the wardrobe, hoisting each sail in turn to check shape and setting angles. A further 'floating star' spinnaker was added for light airs in smooth water.

On the same day Billy 'Jazz-man' Johnson stepped aboard, who having had a great deal of ocean experience aboard sailing yachts in the South Pacific, was the one crewman to call himself a professional sailor on his

Billy Johnson

application form. Originally from San Francisco, he became *Flyer*'s resident DJ, organizing all the jazz festivals on board. His main task was mast hand in Aedgard's starboard watch, but he also proved to be an excellent helmsman in heavy weather.

One worry that remained in the back of Conny's mind was *Flyer*'s rig. While a spare mainmast was all ready to be flown out from Holland, should the spar ever break, he realized that a catastrophe like this would end all chances of winning the Whitbread Trophy, for the time lost making port and fitting the replacement could never be made up again. While looking at the rigs of other racing yachts that had ventured across the Southern Oceans, he dispatched Simon Willis to Los Angeles to make a detailed examination of Jim Kilroy's famous maxi racer *Kialoa* and check on her spar sizes, spinnaker pole end fittings, halyards and winches. Simon brought back reassuring news, for much of *Flyer*'s rig was found to be of the same specifications as on this much larger yacht, and since *Kialoa* had suffered no great damage during her crossing to Australia there was obviously little likelihood that *Flyer* would either.

During his stay in Marblehead Cornelis was able to fulfil an ambition that most yachtsmen hold dear – to sail aboard a modern Twelve Metre. Invited to join a tuning session with Ted Hood aboard his *Independence*, he jumped at the chance and even steered the boat for awhile. 'That was a real

Ari Steinberg

thrill for me', he told Ted afterwards. 'Now I know why there is such mystique attached to these boats.'

Ari Steinberg was another American recruit to sign up in Marblehead, but initially was only interested in a berth in the Transatlantic Race. Just nineteen at the time, this cheerful American had plans to join up with Clare Francis and *ADC Accutrac*, but was later turned down because of his tender age. It was to be Clare's loss, for Ari, young though he was, proved to be tough, and such an asset on board that Cornelis had no hesitation in keeping him on for the big event. Nothing scared him, and he liked it best at the top of the mast in a force 8 gale – and preferably at night!

Cornelis was also keen to have a doctor on board, and remembering a young Dutch student he had sailed with on a friend's yacht in the Mediterranean two years before, he contacted him again. Bert Dykema had the least amount of sailing experience among the crew, but what appealed to Conny most was his zeal to learn and accomplish everything he set out to do. Final studies precluded 'Doc' from joining *Flyer* until just before the start of the Transatlantic Race, and he almost missed the Whitbread Race completely. After having received his doctorate the day prior to the fleet leaving Portsmouth, an air strike prevented him from flying to England. A mad car dash to catch the last ferry from the Continent saw him aboard just a couple of hours before *Flyer* was due to leave. As part of the starboard watch his role on deck was as winch grinder, but when on duty he was also always busy looking for other jobs to do.

One crewman most determined to race around the world was the twenty-eight year old Frenchman Marcel Laurin. Originally an internal auditor, he went to the extreme of having his appendix taken out for the race, just in case it should stop him from joining. When he applied before the cruise across to America there was just one spare berth – that of cook. 'Oh,' he said, 'I can cook – I can do everything.' And on that self-proclaimed recommendation, and Conny's vague belief that all French people can cook, he was taken on. In truth he had never cooked in his life, though he did his best, producing hot meals on time day in and day out whatever the conditions, and it was to his credit that everyone except the skipper actually put on weight during the race.

During the stay in America, it was arranged for Tom Leutwyler, a well known yacht photographer specializing in aerial shots, to fly over during sailing trials. Unfortunately this coincided with an invitation to twenty of Hood's seamstresses to come for a sail. It was a hot sunny day with quite a swell running, and not wanting the yacht to look like a floating harem those poor girls had to be bottled up below as the photographer clicked away overhead. It was not the most enjoyable day's sail for them, as *Flyer* pitched from wave to wave, and some went home feeling very unwell.

Bruce Ashwood (left)

Marcel Laurin sunning
himself between cooking
sessions.

. . . And no sign of a seamstress anywhere! Leutwyler's aerial photographs were taken while twenty of Hood's girls were cooped up below decks.

It was after another of these short training sessions that a little Dutch girl was waiting at the dockside to greet *Flyer*. She had heard that the yacht belonged to a fellow countryman and wanted to say hello. So pretty was she, however, that the first question one crewman asked, jokingly, was where her mother was. 'My mother is divorced,' came the angelic reply, 'would you like to meet her?' They were all off like a shot, only to find that her mother was already very well looked after by a giant of a man called Bef. He was, in every sense of the word, the biggest lobster man in Marblehead, but luckily a firm friendship began and later he placed a large box of these delicacies aboard just before the start of the Transatlantic Race.

However, one thing that puzzled the crew for some while was the line of poultry he sold alongside his lobsters. The sign board proudly proclaimed 'Lobsters 4 dollars. Chickens 2 dollars.' Americanisms can be such stumbling-blocks to foreigners, and they found out that far from being feathered, the 'chickens' were merely small versions of the same shellfish.

June 18 came round all too soon and *Flyer* made her way to the starting line off Manchester, along with a dozen other yachts to start the race for Plymouth, England. In this, *Flyer*'s inaugural race, she was chiefly competing against two other well known boats quite capable of giving her a very hard race: *Demon*, ex-*Scaramouche*, was first to cross the line, and *Immigrant*, America's Cup winner Ted Turner's old Admiral's Cup boat

Tucking into those delicious lobsters – one of the most memorable aspects of *Flyer*'s stay in Marblehead.

*Tenacious*, was not far behind. *Flyer* was second across, her crew more interested in eating the lobster presented earlier than pole position on the line, but after three hours they had overhauled *Demon* and sailed away. The crew was split into two watches, working four hour spells at night and two six hour watches during the day, which worked well and was retained for the next race.

In the beginning winds remained very shifty, falling away altogether at night, with fog often blotting out all visibility. However, *Flyer* proved that she could work well in these fickle conditions, although as they fought their way out into the Atlantic no one was sure who was in the lead. It was sail change after sail change for the first week, as the winds continually boxed the compass, and Simon Willis worked on finding the optimum sail combinations.

Nearly across, *Flyer* was caught in her first gale; with the wind astern and a heavy spinnaker she began to surf down the waves, exceeding 16 knots at times. This was just the practice the crew needed, and it wasn't long before Cornelis could judge who was good in strong conditions. After thirteen days at sea the winds were at their worst, having built up to a force

9 gale, but *Flyer* romped ahead with three reefs in the main, two in the mizzen, and a heavy reacher. While the storm raged overhead, Conny and those off watch listened to the Wimbledon tennis final between Virginia Wade and the Dutch girl Betty Stöve, and couldn't help but laugh at the partisan reporting by the BBC commentator. 'Virginia's playing beautifully . . . oh, brilliant stroke played . . . fast cross-court pass . . . backhand return . . . tremendous pass down the line . . . a lob . . . oh, fantastic smash, Virginia . . .' Poor Betty Stöve was under-rated: whenever she hit a winner it was 'Oh, lucky shot . . . Virginia stood no chance.' But whenever she lost a point it was always because the Dutch girl had been beaten by Virginia's brilliant play.

The next day, July 2, *Flyer* was left with just 274 miles to go and gale warnings all round. Far from what was forecast, they were left totally becalmed and it was another two days to the finish line. Nevertheless it was still a fast crossing of fifteen days, which was enough to give them line honours and the Transatlantic Race on corrected time.

As a prelude to the Round the World Race, this event proved to be invaluable. Everyone knew they had a boat that was strong, fast and controllable in heavy weather racing. Not only did the win give a real boost to morale, but so much had been learned. Cornelis now knew which crew members had the right potential in terms of skill and temperament, what changes had to be made to the boat, and probably most important, he and the basis of his crew now knew how to sail her fast.

In all, there were over a hundred points for Wolter Huisman's yard to alter and correct when *Flyer* was taken back to Vollenhove immediately afterwards. The foredeck hands had continually tripped over the high forehatch, often hidden by a loose sail on deck, so the coaming had to be cut down. Below decks the shower facilities and one of the heads were taken out to leave more space for sail stowage. The crew always used the bumpkin on the stern rather than the toilet below. Four mizzen spinnaker halyards worn through at the exit box at the top of the mast during the race highlighted the continual problem of chafe on halyards, pole end fittings, sheets and control lines, which still had to be rectified. A second tunable radio receiver had to be fitted, to be used with a Morse decoder to obtain weather information transmitted only in Morse code. There was a new radio antenna and backstay. The yard also unstepped and derigged the mast to check it over and weld on some of the stainless steel fittings as an added precaution.

After the Transatlantic Race it had been decided to order a new mainsail to replace the original that had by now crossed the Atlantic twice and was looking a little the worse for wear. Though all Hood sails are described in detail on record cards which are sent to all the company's lofts around the world, the replacement was ordered from Marblehead. This data bank is an excellent idea when it works, but this time it didn't.

Though Simon Willis had already decided to leave *Flyer*, he stayed to help with the final preparations at Hamble – fortunately. When the new sail arrived just before the Fastnet Race he took one look at it, turned to Conny, and said 'No, it's not right. It's nothing like the one I made: you must send it back.' The Marblehead loft had more or less followed the measurements of the original sail, but details of fittings, reinforcements, control lines, etc were quite different. Hood's management insisted that Willis was mistaken and that the sail was an exact replica, and refused to do anything more about it, even refusing to accept the word of two of their own experts, Simon and Adrian Ford, as to its deficiencies. It was left to these two sailmakers to see what they could do on their own, and taking it into the Lymington loft they attempted to re-cut the leech and alter the finishing details into something more like the original. When it was hoisted again, however, it was still far from satisfactory, but with so little time left before the Fastnet, Conny decided to have the old sail patched up and to order another replacement, not from Hood this time but from North Sails, to be sent out to Cape Town. The rogue main was handed back to Hoods at Lymington with a long list of defects that had to be rectified, and it was arranged that it too would be sent out in time for the start of the second leg.

Jerry Dijkstra

Rod White (left) and Chris Moselen

There were three more crew to find, including at the last minute a navigator, and it was only during Cowes Week that Cornelis finally found the man he wanted in Gerard (Jerry) Dijkstra, well known for having raced the Ocean 71 *Second Life* and his own yacht *Bestevaer* in previous Singlehanded Transatlantic Races. Although only learning to sail at the age of twenty, he soon became an accomplished sailor and good tactician, but above all an excellent navigator. He also proved to be a first-class leader, taking over the port watch from Simon Willis.

Another to join the team, two weeks before the start from Portsmouth, was Chris Moselen, a thirty-one year old New Zealander who was probably the strongest man on board. Always with a smile on his face, he acted as foredeck hand with the starboard watch, but is also a very good helmsman and proved to be a great asset on the two heavy weather Southern Ocean legs.

Rod White was the last to step aboard for the race, joining the crew after the Fastnet Race as a reject from *Debenhams*. By this time all the specific jobs had been allocated. However, after spending a great deal of his time below decks, folding sails for the port watch, he was soon to come up with his own label: 'the best bloody sail packer of 'em all.' He also turned out to be a very good helmsman, especially in heavy weather, and kept spirits up with stories and practical jokes. John Ridgway's discard was *Flyer*'s gain.

With the crew complete, it was now time to concentrate on final plans for the real race. Satisfied that *Flyer* was now in top gear, with all the bugs sorted out, Conny's main worry was crew compatibility. Would the new recruits blend in with the existing crew? How would they stand up over a long period of time to the cramped conditions and the demand for constant top performance?

Racing round the world can be compared to climbing Everest, trekking to the South Pole, or exploring the upper reaches of the Zambezi, for each endeavour demands meticulous planning, first-class individual skills and knowledge, but most important a cohesive and functioning team. Arguments or discontent within the group quickly destroy morale and any chance of success. That round the world races accentuate crew problems is one of the less realized facts; usually little is said to non-competitors about things that have happened – tensions, bad atmospheres, cliques, breakdown in the accepted structure of authority on board, even fights or disruptive and tactlessly conducted affairs within crews. Yet compatibility has an immense effect on one's enjoyment of the event, on competitive drive, and on safety.

One of the reasons for sailing across the Atlantic and racing back had been to find those who got on well with others, who could be relied upon to pull their weight, and who were consistently and effectively keen. Any who didn't fit this requirement were weeded out. To an outsider, 'special regulations' posted up in the saloon, together with an unwritten code of conduct, which among other things banned swearing and any criticism of the food, may have seemed a little Teutonic; however, it was this strong disciplinarian code and a strict but fair leadership that kept the *Flyer* team together, for the crew, far from resenting the restrictions, accepted them at face value, realizing why they were required. The rules were not to inhibit enjoyment of the race, and did in fact tighten the bond and comradeship between the crew to such an extent that most have indicated that they would gladly join up and do such a race again together.

Others in the event have been quick to criticize the form of leadership aboard *Flyer* as excessively harsh and not of this time, but no-one can argue with the fact that it worked when the more free and easy attitudes aboard other boats failed, resulting in a loss of sailing efficiency, with personal relationships degenerating into minor feuds in some cases. The strict code aboard *Flyer* kept the crew working as a team with everyone pulling their full weight. Of course there were times when individual habits irritated the others, but the crew quickly learned to keep their mouths shut because everyone aboard realised they were racing on a winner and none wanted to ruin their chances with petty squabbling. Although Conny never had trouble with any of the boys while at sea, there is a limit to the amount of

time anyone can bottle up their emotions, and ashore, when discipline was relaxed, it was perfectly natural for arguments to build up – and they did. But at each port of call everyone was encouraged to take a complete break away from the boat once work was completed, so that they could all let off steam. Also, while relationships between skipper and crew were always very friendly and open-hearted, Conny made a point of never getting involved emotionally or allowing an insight into his personal thoughts or private life.

The common language on board was English, though the skipper and his two Dutch watch leaders often used their native tongue when discussing tactics. None of the others except Bert Dykema could understand what was being said, which no doubt was intended at times, and in a sort of mock rebuke they were quickly nicknamed the Three Commissars, with Conny, Jerry and Aedgard known to the crew thoughout the race as 'Blockheads 1, 2 and 3' respectively.

After competing in an ignominious Fastnet Race, beset by fickle winds and flat calms throughout, *Flyer* arrived at Portsmouth far from favourite for overall honours. Her buildup campaign had been kept very quiet, and few yachting people or journalists knew anything of this Cornelis van Rietschoten, who had not sailed competively for fifteen years. Also, *Flyer* was the only yacht in the race not to have sought or received either

Ramon Carlin, winner of the first Whitbread Race with his Swan 65 *Sayula II*, had some last-minute tips to offer at Portsmouth. He inspected the spinnaker pole end fittings and later Conny changed them from Barient to Sparcraft on his advice. Ramon even ordered the replacements in the USA.

Eight o'clock on the morning
of the start and *Condor*'s crew
are still rigging their
experimental mast.

sponsorship or financial help from suppliers, and many wondered openly whether an amateur entry such as this could compete on equal terms with professionals.

The early favourite was the 77 ft cold-moulded wood *Heath's Condor* designed by John Sharp and co-skippered by the experienced Robin Knox-Johnston and Leslie Williams. She was hampered by having been launched only a little more than a month before and hurriedly prepared: her crew were still fitting spreaders to her mast on the morning of the start!

Some other yachts which were to start off Southsea on August 27 were using the event more as an adventure than a race. *Great Britain II*, at 77 ft 2 in the largest yacht in this race, had a mixed and inexperienced crew (except for the skipper), each having paid £4000 for the privilege of sailing aboard. John Ridgway, who had once rowed the Atlantic with Chay Blyth, was treating his circumnavigation in *Debenhams* as an extension of his outward-bound school in Scotland, and the twelve students aboard *Japy-Hermes* were using the trip as an opportunity to research into life-saving techniques, a part of their college curriculum at the Marseilles College of Engineering.

To the knowledgeable the real challenge seemed to come from *Kings Legend*, a sloop-rigged Swan 65 with a stern modified to improve downwind performance. Her owner-skipper Nick Ratcliffe claimed to have the best boat, sails and crew, which included hardened professional delivery skippers. However, they spent little time sailing together, for after setting off on a tune-up cruise to the Caribbean the winter before, *KL* lost her mast in the Bay of Biscay and the remaining months were spent arguing with Nautor over the responsibility for replacement. Consequently they never worked into a team, and had not established how the boat would be sailed. Cost was another problem that was to plague them throughout the race.

A further real threat came from the 57 ft *Gauloises II*, an aluminium ketch owned by Eric Tabarly and skippered in this race by Eric Loizeau. Although ten years old, she is an extremely fast boat, having won two Sydney–Hobart classics and a Fastnet Race as *Pen Duick III* (with a schooner rig). She would be helped in this event by a large age allowance, giving her one of the most favourable handicaps.

Another boat which was expected to do well was the third French yacht, *33 Export*, a 56 ft André Mauric design built originally to compete (successfully) in the 1968 Singlehanded Transatlantic Race; she had also done the first Whitbread Race four years before. Since then she had been changed from a ketch to a seven-eighths sloop rig, and was now skippered by twenty-three year old Alain Gabbay.

*Adventure* was also doing this race for the second time. A stock fibreglass

The Royal Navy yacht
*Adventure*, with joint British
Armed Services crews.

Nicholson 55, she finished second to *Sayula* and would have undoubtedly won the first WRTWR with a Royal Navy crew had she not had trouble with her rudder during the second leg. This time she was to be sailed by a joint Services crew which (as before) was changed for each leg to give the maximum number of people a chance to join the race.

*B & B Italia* arrived rather unprepared from some races in the Mediterranean with a young and inexperienced crew who had not been with her very long. They found a crack in the mast and changed it two days before the start; this was only possible because a spare Two Ton section was available after the Admiral's Cup series in August.

There were two other Swan 65s in the race, both ketches. These are fibreglass production boats built in Finland to a high standard, although they were never designed for races of this type and are more usually bought as well-built fast cruising yachts. However, there is not a great choice of production yachts in this size that might be suitable for long-distance heavy weather racing, and this fact as well as *Sayula*'s success has contributed to their prevalence in round the world races. *Disque d'Or* was built in 1973, and a Swiss entry skippered by Pierre Fehlmann (whose *Gauloises I* sank in mid-Atlantic in the 1976 OSTAR) with a crew largely made up of dinghy racing enthusiasts. Her sister ship was *ADC Accutrac*, built in 1974, and skippered by Clare Francis, the darling of the British media who had sprung to fame after a singlehanded Atlantic passage followed by the 1976 OSTAR in which she set a world record for women with a twenty-nine day crossing.

Two other boats which looked promising were the French 59 ft masthead sloop *Neptune*, also aluminium and designed specifically for the race by André Mauric, and *Traité de Rome*, ex-*Pinta*, formerly in the winning German Admiral's Cup team and chartered from her owner Willi Illbruck to the Brussels-based Sail for Europe organization. *Neptune*'s skipper was a French yachting journalist, Bernard Deguy, who had competed in both previous round the world races, first on *Pen Duick VI* with Tabarly and then aboard *Kriter*. *Traité de Rome*'s participation was to commemorate the twentieth anniversary of the European Economic Community and as such she carried the unique sail number EUR 1. At 51 ft 2 in she was the smallest boat in the race, and something of a dark horse; while a known performer in ordinary short-race trim, no-one knew how fast she would be carrying stores for the five or six weeks of each leg.

The only other Dutch yacht in the race was *Tielsa*, sponsored by a kitchen-furnishing company. She was built in steel and intended for eventual charter work rather than racing, and carried a higher rating than *Flyer*, which is almost 2 ft longer: she was not expected to perform that well on handicap.

For their part, *Flyer* and her crew were now fully ready for the starter's cannon. Everything had been meticulously planned, and like Paavo Nurmi with his stopwatch, Conny hoped that their departure from Portsmouth would be the start of their timed sprint to the finish.

For purposes of comparison, the following table lists all the competing yachts in order of their IOR rating.

|  | LOA | LWL | Displacement | IOR rating |
|---|---|---|---|---|
| *Heath's Condor* | 77' | 63' | 40 T | 68.8 |
| *Great Britain II* | 77' 2" | 68' 2" | 32.6 T | 68.4 |
| *Tielsa* | 63' 4" | 52' 8" | 27 T | 50.0 |
| *Flyer* | 65' 2" | 49' 9" | 24.6 T | 48.4 |
| *Kings Legend* | 64' 6" | 47' | 25.6 T | 48.4 |
| *ADC Accutrac* | 64' 6" | 47' | 25.6 T | 46.9 |
| *Disque d'Or* | 64' 6" | 47' | 25.6 T | 46.2 |
| *Japy-Hermes* | 62' 2" | 45' 5" | 30 T | 45.1 |
| *Neptune* | 59' 5" | 46' 5" | 21.1 T | 44.7 |
| *B & B Italia* | 54' | 43' 7" | 17.5 T | 41.5 |
| *Debenhams* | 56' 1" | 42' 6" | 18.4 T | 41.3 |
| *33 Export* | 56' 4" | 42' 10" | 12 T | 39.7 |
| *Gauloises II* | 56' 8" | 48' 9" | 13.4 T | 38.1 |
| *Adventure* | 55' | 39' 2" | 17.8 T | 37.5 |
| *Traité de Rome* | 51' 2" | 35' 1" | 13 T | 35.7 |

*Gauloises II, ex Pen Duick III.*

# South through
# the Atlantic

'Fifteen seconds.'

'Free sheets – we're moving too fast.'

Ten . . . five . . . four . . . three . . . two . . . one . . . BANG – roared the ageing cannon from Southsea Castle, fired by Ramon Carlin, winner of the previous Whitbread/RNSA Round the World Race.

Les Williams had *Heath's Condor* across the line first, on a well-timed run with the spinnaker pulling. *Flyer* was eight seconds late, having had to ease sheets after running in too fast. As she crossed, *Great Britain II* luffed hard into the wind to force us up. Rob James, her skipper, is a dinghy sailor at heart and always keen on a good scrap near the line, even in a 77-footer. In fact, it was the same at the start to every leg of this race, but after his near-collision we always kept clear of him. When there are seven thousand miles to race to Cape Town, does it really matter if you are a few seconds late?

Out of the fifteen boats *Flyer* was fourth across. Not too bad, but we had to fight a passage through the two thousand strong spectator fleet, all sounding their horns in salute, with some passing dangerously right across our bows to get a last good look. Jaap van Eesteren was there with his yacht *Atalanta*, carrying family and friends and boldly displaying two giant signs, '*Flyer* Fly Fast' and '*Flyer* Finish First'. We could but do our best.

Rounding Bembridge Ledge buoy on that August 27th, the skies began to brighten and we continued to hold our place behind *Condor*, *GB II* and *Kings Legend*. *Atalanta* gave us a final whistle and wave, and we were on our own. We were racing at last. Everybody aboard was in jubilant spirits: after all the fun and games in Portsmouth we wanted to get down to business, some of us having planned this moment for more than a year. However, heading down the English Channel, spinnaker pulling hard and spray flying, disaster almost overtook us on the first night.

'Boat dead ahead!' was the cry from the foredeck. The wheel spun to starboard. Thank God, we missed by only the smallest fraction. One could have jumped the gap. It was a yacht making heavy weather of the beat back into head seas, and she wasn't showing lights. We only hoped that they were

as scared of the consequences as we had been: a collision would probably have put us out of the race. She passed close by but we couldn't read the name, and then she disappeared into the murk of the night, still without lights.

After sailing across the Bay of Biscay we were frustratingly becalmed off Cape Finisterre. There was not a sail to be seen anywhere on the horizon. Had the others escaped? There was just no way of knowing. But suddenly *GB II* sailed into view, her distinctive sail plan showing up clearly, and

Seconds after the start and *GB II* starts to luff hard, while *Traité de Rome* follows in our wake.

Racing neck and neck with *Neptune* through the armada of yachts that had braved the weather to see us all off.

then there was another yacht: could that be *Kings Legend*? While some of the crew squinted through glasses to see, a school of whales suddenly appeared spouting proudly ahead of us. I was at the wheel and spotted them first through a gap between the sails. I wasn't sure what I had seen at first, but instinctively headed up to avoid them. The school swam within twenty metres off to starboard, but one, more inquisitive than the rest, dived right under the boat to come up close on the port side. The thrash of its tail could have torn away our rudder, and if it had come up under us *Flyer* would have been in serious trouble. But eventually it swam back to the others to bring a great deal of relief on board.

The light winds remained with us for a week and it was a frustrating time. One minute *Flyer* was reaching, slowly building up speed, then the

Clear of the spectator fleet at last and running down the Channel.

Oh dear! One of the early problems in the race.

next the wind would be right on our nose. At one point we could do no more than eight miles in eight hours, changing sails constantly to try to catch every last ounce out of what breeze there was. By this time there were no yachts on the horizon, and the big worry was that the rest of the fleet might have escaped the calms. So far, there had been little radio contact and relative positions were vague. We just had no way of knowing.

Whales continued to appear from time to time; they could have been finbacks but no-one was sure. On the seventh night in particular we could hear them blowing all around and could smell them – just like bad fish at a market – but oddly enough their smell seemed stronger at night than during daytime.

Despite the many sail changes, for some reason our spinnaker handling was appalling and stupid mistakes were being made all the time. On one occasion we put the spinnaker pole right through the bottom of the sail during a gybe, and kept tearing the flimsy material on almost every peel. The race wasn't going to be won this way, I thought, but the problem was that it had taken longer than I expected for the three crew changes made after the Atlantic race to settle down. It ended with us fearing every gybe and spinnaker peel, and instead we would hold on to an unfavourable course, or change bald-headed.

By the eighth day *Kings Legend* was fifty miles ahead and *Disque d'Or*, which raced under a lower handicap than ours, was also leading us. Both were sailing in better winds. Adrian still had work to do below, repairing the mistakes made in previous changes. This reluctance to gybe cost us dearly for while we were forced to tack and keep clear of Madeira most of the other yachts sailed well to the east for a shorter route. Luck was with us, however, because we had a fairly fast reach past the island while the other two yachts had a slower course dead downwind.

By this time Hugh Wilson was showing a hidden talent. Wielding a spanner was not his only mètier, and bringing out a pair of scissors he set up a barber shop on deck. So impressed were some by the results that we thought he might start up a diary for appointments! I was among those to decline. One look at each of those shorn sheep was more than enough to make me wait five weeks for a Cape Town trim!

Little had been heard from *Heath's Condor* since the start. Her radio receiver had stopped working soon after leaving the English Channel, but the problem was only transmitted back to Race Control as the yacht passed close to the Spanish coast where Les Williams could use the short-range VHF set on board to broadcast his message through a local Spanish station. Though required by the race rules for safety reasons, at the time the faulty radio had made little difference to *Condor*'s performance, and by the Canaries she was well up on the rest of the fleet and lying third on handicap. However, she was fast approaching the Doldrums and needed accurate weather forecasts to choose the quickest path through.

Back in Britain, Robin Knox-Johnston, her co-skipper, moved heaven and earth to get a replacement radio aboard. In the end he got special dispensation from the Race Committee to use a helicopter and lower a new receiver down into a rubber dinghy towed behind the yacht as she passed Las Palmas. It saved a day in port, but in the end it didn't save the race. A little while later their special carbon reinforced fibreglass mast snapped in two places as the yacht crashed through a wave in twenty knots of wind. This high-technology spar had offered weight-saving advantages, but the boat's short pre-race trial period had not included any realistic testing of what was really an experimental design.

The close-sheeted mizzen
genoa.

At the same time, the French yacht *33 Export*, well-tried and another of the early favourites, was also experiencing problems. She had to put into Madeira to replace a rigging screw that had been lost overboard, and later her engine room was flooded by a big wave that came in via the cockpit and left the engine full of salt water. This made it impossible to keep the batteries charged for transmitting. Little was heard from her crew for the rest of the first leg and these delays finished their chances of winning the race. Compared with all this, our few blown-out spinnakers were chicken feed!

Midway through the second week the *Flyer* boys were beginning to gain confidence and sail changes were much improved. Conditions were steadily changing to suit us. We had pulled back to within eight miles of *Kings Legend*, and *Disque d'Or* was now twenty-miles astern. The winds had changed to produce light reaching conditions which favoured *Flyer*'s special ketch rig. Olin Stephens had specified short-length spreaders for her mizzenmast; the shrouds ran to inboard chainplates on the deck and the reduced effective angle was compensated for by a heavier mast section. The rig allowed the mizzen genoa to be set with as little as 60° apparent wind angle on the instruments. This sail could be used to good effect in anything up to force 5 and when set would immediately add a knot to boat speed. It was a real advantage to us in light conditions like these and when carrying it *Flyer* would often outpace the sloop-rigged *Kings Legend* by fifteen to twenty miles a day. This was our secret weapon and was to pay handsome dividends throughout the race. We never kept to a strict course but sailed to the wind for maximum speed while constantly adjusting sail trim. Jerry had drawn up a Vmg table, listing wind angles and comparative speeds that had to be achieved to sail the optimum courses. It may have given him as navigator a few headaches, but the tactics paid off. Every course change was written down in the log at the time, so that there was a constant record, the responsibility of the watch on deck.

On the twelfth day our first flying fish came on deck. The experts say they taste like herring but have more bones: we never had the chance to find out. Marcel, in sole charge of the cuisine, preferred to prepare the freeze-dried foods that we had on board. For those he had just to add boiling water – but these flying fish – well, they came without any instructions at all – let alone in French!

But if the flying fish were a lost delicacy, the crew weren't too worried. They had more important matters to worry about. An innocent chess game between Jerry and Aedgard, the two watch leaders, soon developed into a full-scale battle of wits with one watch fighting to steal honours from the other. It was played during lunch and dinner times and lasted ten days. For the crew off watch the match proved the biggest topic of conversation as they plotted their game ten moves ahead. Very often a few of the pieces

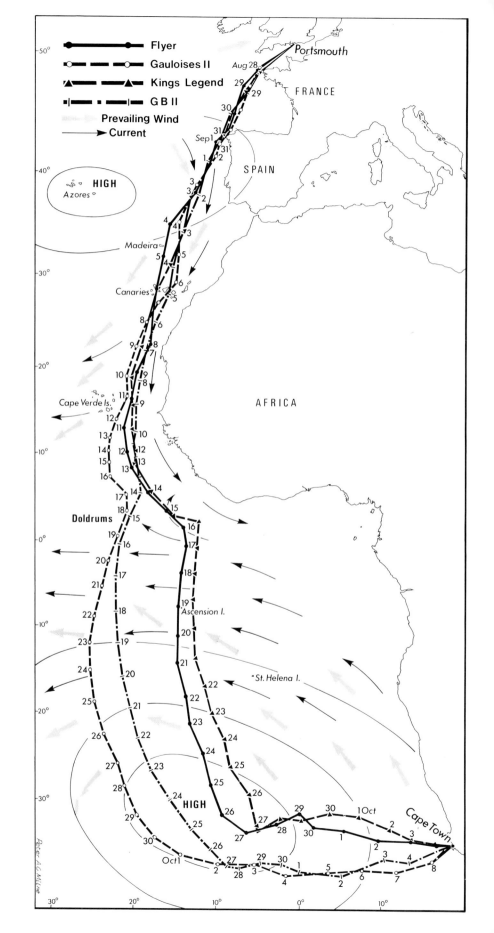

never quite found their way back to their previous squares, but any advantage gained by this was probably lost because the crew on deck always had an ear to the hatches and ventilation system to catch snippets of intelligence about the long-term tactics of the opposition. It was all great fun, and through fair means and foul Jerry's watch eventually won.

On the thirteenth day the winds had started to pick up, rising to force 6 at times. *Flyer* began to live up to her name, averaging nine or ten knots, leaping through the waves and leaving a wild trail of foam astern. It was exhilarating sailing in glorious weather. Now we were heading for the Doldrums, that area dividing North and South Atlantic and notorious for its fickle winds. We had set a course that many of the clipper ships favoured in the past, and which *Adventure*, the winning boat on this leg in 1973, had taken. We could only hope for the same fair winds that she had enjoyed, helping her to break through in less than three days.

This fine run was interrupted by a bang. I looked up to see the .75 oz spinnaker blown to shreds – Adrian had another chance to ply his trade. We had left this light sail hoisted in too strong a wind, but eight hours later Adrian had those tattered pieces patched together and stitched back into the leech tapes to make a spinnaker once more.

That evening we contacted Nick Ratcliffe aboard *Kings Legend*, who called back, 'What's the price of whisky now?' The significance of this was that our three-boat team, which included *Disque d'Or*, was now well in the running for the Team Prize and a keg of Long John Scotch.

The winds had now moved dead astern and in these conditions *Kings Legend* was definitely faster, for with her taller rig and bigger spinnaker she carries more sail area. But we had logged another 210 miles in the day and were doing much better than the other Swan 65s in this race. We were also gaining time on the smaller boats as we approached the Doldrums; our light air downwind tactic of sailing a zig-zag course to create our own wind, rather than going on a dead run, was paying handsome dividends. Our sail handling was also coming right, and spinnakers were no longer being torn when gybing. However, we were all concentrating so hard on building up *Flyer*'s speed that no-one noticed the slow but steady increases in wind strength. There was another sharp report aloft and our light spinnaker blew out once more. It was another lesson learned, but on the foredeck hands were quick to pull down the remnants and set the heavier kite. *Flyer* was never without sail for long.

By the fifteenth day the winds were getting very light and fickle, the air hot and humid. It was like an oven on board but we had to keep up boat speed at all costs. Winds varied from almost nothing to force 4 and sail changes were frequent. Light, then medium and finally heavy sails were set, and quickly dropped again to suit the ever-dying breeze. When

'Down spinnaker' and within seconds it would be swallowed up below.

changing spinnakers we would hoist the new sail inside the one already up so that we were never without sail, then peel the outer one away just before the inner spinnaker had filled. However, sometimes when a heavier spinnaker was hoisted and filled before the outer sail had been peeled away, it would press the light sail out of its leeches. That day we damaged yet another sail this way, and I then made the decision to go bald-headed, dropping one spinnaker before hoisting the other. We lost speed during the time when there was no sail up, but we didn't keep tearing spinnakers!

*Kings Legend* was the first to hit the Doldrums and reported her position to be twenty-five miles ahead, but more to the east. Our light-air tactics were certainly paying off and had halved the distance between us. On the radio that night we found that the other two Swans, *ADC Accutrac* and *Disque d'Or*, were more than eighty miles astern, and that *GB II* was just over the horizon five miles ahead. We were still shy-reaching, running through the water at eight knots with just seven knots of wind across the deck, thanks to our ketch rig. There were just two topics of conversation aboard at the time – sex and boat speed – but when we heard that *KL* was so little ahead, girls were soon forgotten, for a while at least!

We still managed to run 186 miles that day, and hit the Doldrums the following morning. This was where we needed the luck. Yachts can sit in this part of the Atlantic for four or five days waiting for a fresh breeze, and in this race it would probably mean the difference between being first or an

also-ran. We were completely becalmed for two and a half hours. The heat
and humidity were so intense that it was like sitting in a hothouse. At last
the wind picked up again from the west and with it came a tropical
rainstorm – the first real shower since leaving Portsmouth. The cool fresh
water was such a relief that everyone came up on deck naked with soap in
hand ready to have a wash, and it was our first bath in fresh water for nearly
three weeks. The clouds rolled away, the winds held and we were sailing in
sunshine at seven knots. It was glorious weather, but our luck ran out later
in the day. The winds died again to leave us virtually becalmed for more
than thirteen hours, although we never quite lost steerage way. We were all
working hard, steering to the wind, trimming and changing headsails
constantly to suit the zephyrs that came in from all directions, and trying to
maintain a little boat speed.

Our big break came late in the eighteenth day. *Flyer* was drenched by
another tropical storm, but along with the rain came wind. We changed to a
light reacher, then soon after to a heavier flanker as the wind direction
changed. The boat moved ahead like an express train, belting along at ten
knots, water flying across the deck. She was overcanvased, and in tempting
luck we were rewarded with a vicious broach. Not many crews can say they
broached in the Doldrums!

Later in the day we spotted another whale, and this time a massive one.

Becalmed in the Doldrums.

It swam in a half-circle around the boat taking a good look at us. I had never seen one of these mammals so clearly before; after showing its markings it spouted a farewell and dived away.

By the next day the fun was over and *Flyer* was back in light airs again with the rain finally dying out after an eight-hour downpour. The one consolation was that once the clouds had rolled back we were able to dry our clothes and gear in the warm sun. However good waterproof clothing is it can never keep out torrential rain, and once penetrated it quickly soaks through everything underneath. It is a clammy, uncomfortable feeling with underclothes sticking to the skin as you move about, but there is nothing that can be done. If one changes clothes, they too are quickly wet through as well, and we just had to sit it out and wait for sun. However, the rains had not dampened the enthusiasm aboard, for *Flyer* was first through the Doldrums, having been becalmed for no more than a day. Marcel was the only one to have a problem. There was a terrible smell in the galley, and although we joked about his socks he eventually discovered that it was the cheese that had gone bad in the humid heat, and it all had to be turned over the side.

Here, as we closed the Equator, the tactics for the remainder of the leg had to be decided. Should we take the longer 'clipper route' and enjoy the fresh reaching winds all the way round to Cape Town, or the short cut directly south and head into the Southeast Trades? In the last WRTWR the ketches and downwind machines struck a course well to the west, reaching down below this area of highs, and sailed under spinnakers all the way to Cape Town. But we decided to follow the course set by *Adventure* in that race and cut the corner. *Flyer*'s short upper mainmast spreaders enabled us to sheet genoas in hard, and she had already proved herself to be more efficient on the wind than the other ketches in this race, especially the two Swans, and could even out-sail our immediate rival, the sloop-rigged *Kings Legend*, in certain conditions.

Steady southeasterlies eventually arrived on our twenty-first day at sea. With the changing wind came an equally sudden change in the weather. The air was now dry, the sky overcast, and at last those flying fish had vanished. The daily radio link, prearranged by the skippers, continued to show us all sailing on different headings, and it was far too soon to know how these tactics would work out.

The morning after, news came via the radio that *Condor* had broken her fibreglass mast. It was a quick end for this early favourite, who now had to sail under jury rig for Monrovia in Liberia to collect an aluminium replacement, already constructed and ready to be flown out from Britain in three sections. The delay forfeited her chance of winning the leg, and very probably the whole race. For her crew it was a disappointing end to the

Navigating with the more sophisticated electronic position finding systems, or the use of weather facsimile equipment, was not allowed. Here we see the 400 watt Sirius receiver/transmitter on the left, with radio direction finder. At top right is a Sony synthesized shortwave receiver used with the Pickering Morse decoder underneath. The decoder converted Morse transmissions into conventional numbers and letters which appeared in the display window. Other equipment includes a Dancom VHF transceiver, barograph, ELAC deep-water echosounder, and Brookes & Gatehouse sailing instruments. A tape recorder was used to try to slow down high-speed Morse weather signals.

race, but they continued to sail, joining up with the rest of the fleet in Cape Town well before we all left on the second leg.

The radio net was a purely informal arrangement between competitors and had nothing to do with the twice-weekly position reports to Race Control at Portsmouth. The idea was a safety precaution but helped to relieve the boredom and stress that can build up when sailing for long periods in isolation, and proved to be a very sensible arrangement. Not only did it allow crews the chance to see if they had gained or lost ground on the opposition during the previous twenty-four hours, but gave us the comfort of knowing that medical advice or assistance was on call should the need ever arise – provided that one's radio worked. Apart from the obvious safety aspect in frequent position reports, this contact also helped to stimulate the sense of competition when one's opponents were almost always out of sight. After an initial reluctance in the first days out from England, there was some mutual suspicion of other boats listening but not reporting, particularly weather; also some misleading position reports from boats which felt they were supplying tactical information. Trans-

missions ranged from voluble to minimal.

The next day, Saturday the seventeenth, we crossed the Equator on port tack, sailing for speed. Billy Johnson, a keen fancy-dress partygoer, wanted to dress up in the sailors' tradition as old Neptune, but I gave him a signed certificate instead; after all we were racing, not cruising. It wasn't quite the same for him, but we broke out the beer rations for the first time and invited our trident-carrying friend to come to Cape Town to celebrate instead.

A hard sail on the wind now faced us all the way to Cape Town. With decks heeled at 30° life aboard was more difficult, and the constant crashing into waves became an annoyance. There was relatively less to do; sails needed little attention in the steadier windward conditions, sheets were now cleated, and it was left up to the helmsman to get the most out of the boat. However, to help relieve the boredom I decided to change the watch system to give two people twenty-four hours off each day, which they mostly spent reading or sleeping, and this was continued all the way to Cape Town.

However, Jerry was getting very worried about the high pressure system ahead. No weather forecasts were coming through the Pickering Morse decoder, because we had no reception from the Cape Town weather station. But from what we learned from other ships, the so-called steady South Atlantic high was on the move, changing position by as much as 500 miles in 24 hours. If we ran straight into the high instead of skirting round it we could well be left becalmed and lose our lead. The next day we were still no wiser until late afternoon when Clare Francis came in on the regular radio show. The news was mixed. We were still well in the lead, sailing at the same speed as the much larger *GB II* and pulling away slightly from *Kings Legend*, who looked to be more than ninety miles astern with *Disque d'Or* a further 330 miles back. But she had spoken to a passing French ship, which had given her the weather forecast over the radio. (Though literally 'outside assistance', such information was allowed by the race rules as long as it was passed on to all other competitors.) Our worst fears were confirmed: the high was dead ahead. Would it move away in time, or leave us becalmed?

Apart from the weather, the mainsail was causing us trouble too. The stitching on the lower batten pockets was now severely worn from the constant slab reefing, and while Adrian did his best his good work would be undone again in a few days.

*Flyer* was proving to be better in these windward conditions than anyone had dared imagine. With sheets eased a little for optimum speed, we were closehauled at a steady eight or nine knots, 40° off the wind. The motion through the waves was very uncomfortable, but at least each crest was one

Closehauled with spray flying everywhere.

nearer to Cape Town. *Adventure* had averaged 6.7 knots on this leg in the 1973 race, but we were going much faster, which was all very encouraging although we still had the worry of the high up ahead. It was now two days away and the gamble was on.

We ploughed on relentlessly. They were lousy conditions, and with little to do on board but hold on tight it was sometimes difficult to maintain a racing attitude. It was mostly *Kings Legend'* position astern that kept us going hard. While the crew might have been feeling the strain, *Flyer* was enjoying every moment, pounding her way through the seas at the rate of 200 miles a day. During the past five days we had covered 1,060 miles and were steadily pulling away from the fleet with only *KL* in a position to beat us.

Jerry was at last picking up weather reports from Cape Town – the Morse decoder was working well – and these confirmed that this elusive high was not at all in its normal place. It was a worrying time. We assumed from her earlier position report that *Kings Legend* was to the north of us, about the same distance away from Cape Town. It was all very close, and I just hoped that we were in a better position to take advantage of the expected westerly freeing our wind first, without running into that high. Jerry struggled with our receiver, trying to pick up the Cape Town weather reports and pinpoint the calms, but just when we needed the information most, atmospherics blotted out all reception, as had probably happened

The electric sewing machine could be fitted into the passageway between the two forward cabins, and here Adrian Ford spent many hours mending the sails.

previously. The wind appeared to be backing a little: could the high be coming back across our path? It was a pessimistic thought, but a strong possibility. If the wind stayed as it was, our position as leader was in jeopardy: *Kings Legend* would have been closer to Cape Town. What we badly needed was a wind shift.

We decided to tack across to 065° in an effort to consolidate our position towards Cape Town. Shortly afterwards there was a shout from the deck: 'Sail on the horizon!' and it was recognized as *Kings Legend*. As she drew closer it looked as if we could be on converging tacks. Eventually she passed 300 yards ahead and tacked to cover us, but with the seas now very lumpy

*Flyer* moved ahead like a bulldozer, shovelling spray in every direction. We slowly pulled ahead, *Flyer's* finer hull shape making better weather through the rough going than the Swan, and next morning Ari sighted her from the masthead still on the same tack but dropping well back. Their appearance in the middle of the ocean had certainly been incredible, for after sailing hard for four weeks, over a distance of nearly 6,000 miles, there was really nothing to choose between us and it could well prove to be a close finish at Cape Town.

Adrian's fight to save the mainsail was now an almost daily chore, with the sail taken down for restitching. Eventually the batten pockets became quite unrepairable and had to be replaced with completely new material. Every time the sail came down we lost valuable power, although surprisingly in strong winds the speed was very little reduced under genoa and mizzen alone, and it was only in the lulls that we noticed any real difference.

On the thirty-second day we thought our prayers had been answered. The winds became light, there was rain, but, more important, it started to free us: this could be it. But it wasn't, for within three hours the wind direction had swung back again and we were right back to square one. The high was definitely moving back across our path once more and we were forced to put in another tack. We were almost down to the latitude of Cape Town and could only hope that eventually the wind would turn southerly. By midday we found ourselves 180 miles due north of the high and being tracked by a giant albatross – a beautiful bird with a six foot wingspan. Like an enormous plane it never flapped its wings but glided over the waves, sweeping off to one side then the other, and always waiting to be tempted with scraps of food.

But our thoughts were soon brought back to the boat. A rip chased a path across the foot of the genoa, the sail having given up the fight against constant pounding into head winds and seas. The foredeck hands quickly changed down to the no. 2 genoa and Adrian went below to work another miracle, but while he was down there *Kings Legend* put in another appearance. Despite the different tactics and our worries about the high, she had not broken away and it was obviously going to be a tight race over the last 900 miles.

The southeasterly force 6 wind still showed little sign of abating, or even freeing us to a more favoured course. In fact, with the wind backing ESE *Flyer* was headed and we were forced to bear away from Cape Town once more; I began to wonder if we would have this hard windward slog all the way to the finish. Eventually we were headed so far that we had to tack to 165° to keep her on a course anywhere near to Cape Town, but fifteen minutes later we were forced to tack back again. The seas were then very lumpy and with the wind gusting to force 7 at times even managed to stop all headway. We then decided to come about and head south, hoping to reach down towards the easier southwesterly airstream.

The skies had been shrouded in cloud for forty-eight hours or more, and with no chance to take sun or star sights we could only estimate our position. I knew it would be another rough night, but we were again thankful to Huisman for building such a watertight ship, for at least we had dry warm bunks to climb into. Apart from the good hot food that Marcel managed to produce, whatever the weather, they were our only comfort. In contrast, other yachts in this race were full of leaks, leaving few berths without a constant drip from above to provide a cold Chinese water torture for their crews.

It now looked as if we had escaped the high, which instead was tormenting Rob James on *GB II*, who had sailed straight into its centre and was completely becalmed. Our strong headwinds were certainly not comfortable, but they were infinitely better than none at all.

Conditions proved to be just as hard going the next morning, the thirty-fifth day, but the wind had backed and for the first time we could head straight for Cape Town on 100°. Now that we were nearing land, twenty more albatrosses found our wake. Their graceful movements traced tracks like skiers sweeping down a slope, moving first one way, turning, then gliding back. They were to escort us all the way to the Cape.

With them came a freeing wind, allowing us to ease sheets and reach through the seas. The motion became much more tolerable, and after all the crashing and banging of the previous week it was certainly a night to enjoy. On the radio show *Tielsa*, the other Dutch yacht in the race, told us that she was enjoying good freeing winds further west on the 'clipper route' and that her spinnaker had remained set for twelve days.

This wind shift gave *Flyer* a greater advantage than it did *Kings Legend*, which was sailing 90 miles further north with sheets still pinned in hard – although we didn't know this at the time. It was definitely building up to be a nail-biting finish for there was just no way of knowing if our more southerly position would pay off in the end. There were other uncertainties too. Would our lead be sufficient to beat *GB II* boat for boat, and could we also get across the finish at Cape Town with enough extra time to beat *Gauloises II* on handicap? Like *Tielsa*, she had taken the more westerly route and was going fast under spinnaker for the finish. It was all very tight and exciting.

Adding to our anxieties, those batten pockets on the mainsail were now a real aggravation. The winds had slackened and we could no longer afford to keep taking down the sail for repairs. The pockets were virtually gone, and the only answer was to bolt the battens in place through the cloth and just hope they would hold until the finish.

Then we ran into calms. Jerry calculated that we were now less than three days out from Cape Town, yet *Flyer* could hardly make more than six miles in four hours. It became more and more tense as the windless hours ticked by. *Gauloises*, further south, was running at ten knots and eating up our lead every minute. There was just nothing we could do to build up our wake and it was a full twelve hours before *Flyer* could start sailing again. The big worry now was whether *Kings Legend* had run ahead and out of reach. The wait for the radioed positions that night felt more like days than hours. It was a frustrating time, but eventually *Legend* came on the air to tell us that she had taken a course further north and was now eight miles astern. It was good news indeed, bringing immediate relief to tattered nerves and a fresh sense of purpose to our racing. The crew worked extra hard, striving to get every last ounce of power from the sails, and whatever we did – adjust a sheet, change sail, or even throw garbage overboard – brought a new stock phrase: 'Well, that puts us ahead of *KL* again.'

But the same radio show also brought news of our other adversary. *Gauloises* had run 240 miles in the past twenty-four hours, gaining more than eighty miles on us. There was now just a ninety mile stretch of water between us and the finish and we all knew what had to be done if *Flyer* was to save her handicap. It had become a race against time.

At least the calms had been left well astern, and *Flyer* was moving fast in the right direction with a big spinnaker set. We were back to our light air downwind gybing tactics again, making the most of our ketch rig.

The South Africans were now getting keyed up about the race and preparing for the finish. We had a call through Cape Town Radio and an hour after we had given them our position a South African Air Force Shackleton was circling above. *Kings Legend* could be seen astern from Ari's lookout position halfway up the mast, and we continued to gybe downwind, maintaining our fastest course but keeping a careful eye astern. It was all very bad for the nerves but good for the adrenalin!

The last night, however, was the worst. The winds deserted us altogether almost within sight of the finish. *Kings Legend* was suffering the same conditions, but *Gauloises* continued coming fast up from the south. No-one could sleep for wondering what would happen.

Thankfully, our prayers were answered the next morning, October 5. The wind set in and *Flyer* finished in fine style with a two hour and four minute advantage over *Kings Legend*. Nick Ratcliffe was the first to congratulate us over the radio – a gesture well appreciated after the hard fight. We had completed the 6,816 miles at an average speed of 7.1 knots and in a record time of thirty-eight days, twenty-one hours. *Gauloises II* found it impossible to beat this time on handicap, and this very fast French yacht finished third. Fourth on handicap was *Disque d'Or*, to assure us of

A reporter from the Cape Town daily paper asked Conny to pose for a picture after receiving the first prize, promising a print afterwards.

The Wool Board of South Africa presented *Flyer* with a beautiful trophy for taking line honours on the first leg.

the Long John Team Prize, and was followed by *Traité de Rome* and *Adventure*. *GB II*, although third across the finish line, ended up twelfth on handicap once the corrected times had been taken into account.

There to welcome us were those very same banners that had cheered us on our way from Portsmouth. Only this time 'Flyer Fly Fast' and 'Flyer Finish First' decorated the sides of a harbour tug packed with Dutch people. They gave us a fantastic reception, which was second in delight only to my first hot bath in six weeks.

Once the initial parties were over, there were a great many repair jobs to be worked through before our three-week stop was over. The crates of spares packed and sent by Wolter Huisman, and the freeze-dried food and 'fog' bread, had arrived and everybody buckled down to the work in hand. Adrian worked through the sails, replacing reef cringles, adding chafe patches and doing other repairs. The headstay foil came off, and hanks were fastened to the luff tapes of the headsails. Also a spare spinnaker pole and specially designed 2.6 oz spinnaker came aboard, for the anticipated Southern Ocean conditions. The idea was to set this inside the forestay, hoisted on the spare spinnaker pole topping lift. However, conditions never justified the extra weight of this small sail and its equipment and it

Robin Knox-Johnston lying out full stretch while re-rigging *Condor*'s mast gives some scale to the massive spar.

*Heath*'s *Condor*, with *GB II* one of the two maxi-raters in the fleet and racing for line honours as well as on handicap.

*GB II* in drydock showing a large area to scrub clean, which her crew had to do all themselves.

First sight of the Cape of Good Hope and what is to come, as the crew take off for the Etosha game reserve and a well-earned break from the boat.

was left ashore in Auckland. The swivel blocks had broken when used on spinnaker halyards, probably from the combination of heavy load and constant twisting from the movement of the sail; all the winches were overhauled (they gave no trouble during the race). The Barient spinnaker pole end fittings had proved too sharp for the wire afterguys, chewing up the serving and splice practically every four hours or so. We were lucky to get the ends welded up in such a way that the chafe was reduced. However, this did not eliminate the problem completely, and they were eventually replaced with Sparcraft 'bearclaws' in Auckland. These gave much less trouble and rarely opened accidentally, but the screws securing them to the poles had to be tightened regularly.

In Cape Town, Frits Palthe, who organized the repair work on *Flyer*, also had our best interests at heart. Frits's motto was 'nothing but the best' and it applied equally well to both his work on the boat and everything else he arranged. He set up a party that none of us will ever forget – inviting about sixty girls, which was more than enough for those interested on *Flyer*.

In this type of long distance racing crews need to wind down after the pressure and excitement of the event, so once the job list had been ticked off I chartered an ageing DC3 and took crew, along with a party of friends, across Africa on an eight hour flight to the Etosha Pan Game Reserve, not far from the Angola border. In all, we stayed four days and it was a great success. Everyone was able to relax, forget about the racing, and

Vanessa Weinlig from Cape Town, who had sailed on *Sayula II* to the prizegiving in London, enjoys a sail on board *Flyer* during the stay in South Africa.

'I'm Sue from Monday night. Remember me?' Her son gave Conny a tiny panda bear as a lucky charm. Sue was a barmaid at *Flyer*'s host pub in Portsmouth before the start. Inger van Rietschoten was standing just behind.

After one of the many times it dipped in the water, the main boom broke.

Surfing downwind threw up a pronounced stern wave (left).

Foredeck hands fight down the genoa after setting a spinnaker.

Over 15 knots *Flyer*'s speedometer did not read because of aeration, but in conditions like these she often surfed at 20 knots despite the terrific drag of the boom in the water.

The racing fleet tied up in Auckland harbour (right).

The start off Auckland, New
Zealand.

A low-lying iceberg, harder to see than the more spectacular high bergs, and in that sense more dangerous.

Chris Moselen waking his watch leader Adrian Koekebakker, who returned the gesture by filling the same bucket and throwing it in Chris' bunk — then occupied by Ari Steinberg, who was just off watch and asleep.

A welcome home from ships and yachts in Rotterdam's Waterweg.

Crowds waiting near the Royal Maas Yacht Club in Rotterdam.

enjoy the sights and this did much to relieve the tensions that build up in a race like this.

*Heath's Condor* was the penultimate boat and placed last on handicap, and sailed in with a yellow quarantine flag fluttering in the new rigging. It was said that some aboard were suffering from diarrhoea, the ill effects of Monrovian water, but this was a thin disguise quickly unmasked. Unfortunately for them, those ill effects were of a much more personal nature, and with bad news travelling fast most of the girls gave the boat a very wide berth indeed. Such are the pleasures of Monrovian nightlife! At the same time Ted Hood telephoned to congratulate us and ask if there was

One . . . two . . . three . . . HEAVE. *Flyer* about to be relaunched, ready for the second leg to Auckland.

Start day at Cape Town.

anything further his firm could do. Apparently he had not known personally of our problems, and the news that we had now taken a North main on board was like a red rag to a bull. However, the replacement sail altered yet again by Hood Lymington and shipped from England was much nearer the original shape and specifications, and we decided to use it on the second leg. It was certainly better than the original Hood main with its torn batten pockets and a leech that had been stretched almost twenty-four inches by 17,000 miles of hard sailing.

# The Southern Ocean Begins

There were mixed feelings aboard as Cape Town was left astern. A final Dutch party the night before had kept us all out of our beds until early in the morning of October 25th, so no one was in any mood for shouting. Although we got a good start – keeping well clear of Rob James and his dinghy tactics this time – our minds were not really on the race at all. Instead, thoughts lingered on some of the great times had in port, though some wondered what terrors this Indian Ocean leg might hold. The mountainous seas experienced in the first race had claimed three lives, and *Sayula*, the eventual winner, was almost capsized by a giant wave that rolled her down more than 140°. It was a knockdown like this that I dreaded most.

A man-overboard incident was very worrying too, but we had formulated a plan should an emergency like this ever arise, to bring us back within minutes for the pickup. An extra tube through the transom housed the lifebuoy together with a strobe light and transmitter, both of which would be activated the moment they hit the water. This was in addition to the dan buoys stowed in long tubes on either side of the transom. Whoever was on the helm when the alarm was raised had to pull a lever in the cockpit, which opened the flap over the tube and shot the buoy and its equipment straight into the sea, taking one dan buoy with it to mark the spot. Then, while one crewman on deck kept his eyes on the light, another fetched the homing device which would be used to pick up the signals from the floating transmitter and give us a course to steer back.

If we were sailing into the wind at the time, the plan was to gybe, the quickest way to turn round, but if *Flyer* was running with the spinnaker up the afterguy had to be released completely so that the clew of the sail would fly free from the pole and ready to be hauled down quickly before the boat was rounded up into the wind. After having made sure that no ends were trailing in the water, the engine would then be started and the propeller engaged. I estimated that all this could be achieved within 300 metres to give us a reasonable chance of finding the man again before he suffered too much from the cold. Because the engine was run daily for generating

The start of the second leg. Some people look a little tired from the final fling in Cape Town.

Our supporters out to say goodbye to us.

Three tubes through the transom carried the emergency man-overboard markers and transmitter.

purposes, and kept in a maintained state, there should be no difficulty in starting it in an emergency.

We had been warned that it could be tactically risky to sail too close to the shore after leaving Cape Town. In the first race the yachts had been left becalmed at night, so we decided to strike a course six or seven miles offshore. Unfortunately, it was the first of many mistakes we made on this leg; while our position in the fleet must have been quite good as the evening closed in, far from getting wind we lay becalmed, losing all steerage way at times, while those closer inshore made their first break, enjoying a fresh breeze. There we sat over the Agulhas Bank, a notorious sailors' graveyard where westerly storms are supposed to fight against the opposing currents, whipping up the seas to freak heights – yet we were totally becalmed without a ripple showing on the water.

Three days later our position was no better. The crew were slowly gathering their wits and getting into the swing of racing again, but we just couldn't break out of the calm. What was even more disconcerting was the

The smallest yacht in the race, with Philip Hanin at the wheel.

fact that *Disque d'Or* had sailed onto our horizon, and skirted round and past us during the day, sailing in completely different winds. *Flyer* had a private patch of calm all to herself and we could do no more than 70 miles that day while the rest of the fleet stormed on ahead further south. The situation couldn't have been more bleak!

It was a full four days before there was a change, but when the freshening winds eventually came they filled in with a vengeance. *Gauloises* lost her rudder after broaching in a vicious gust further south. This was really bad luck for it left them with little or no chance to take our lead unless both *Kings Legend* and ourselves also had serious trouble. Her crew had changed their rudder in Cape Town for a much stronger one designed and built specifically to withstand the stresses of the Southern Ocean, but they were to find later that its construction was faulty. They were delayed a week and forced to put back to Port Elizabeth and refit the old rudder, which was used without further trouble for the rest of the race.

Disappointment for the crew
of *Gauloises II*, which had to
put into Port Elizabeth to
replace her rudder.

But we had our own problems that day too. After sitting in calms for
almost four days, a sudden squall tore our 1.5 oz medium spinnaker to
shreds. The sail was completely beyond repair. The next night, exactly the
same thing happened again within ten minutes of the time of the previous
evening's episode, but this time it was our heavyweight 2.2 oz spinnaker
that blew out. The winds had suddenly jumped from force 3 to 7 and with
them went the head of the sail. This time, however, it remained attached to
the sheets, so we were able to drag it in over the stern while Ari was hoisted
up the mast to retrieve the halyard.

We were not the only boat to lose sails in these suddenly gusting winds.
*ADC* performed a classic Chinese gybe, broaching first to windward then
to leeward, and although the spinnaker was recovered undamaged, their
best genoa, stored in its bag but untethered on deck, was washed overboard
and lost. Later she was also to blow out her starcut spinnaker leaving just a
small section at the masthead. *Japy-Hermes* also blew her spinnaker along

with the big boy, and *Neptune* broke both spinnaker poles: it was certainly a smashing twenty-four hours.

From the radio show that night, we found that while *Flyer* was in fighting range of *ADC*, *33 Export* and *Traité de Rome*, our main rival *Kings Legend* had streaked ahead and was now running close to the much larger *GB II*. What was worse, however, was the fact that *KL* was following a more southerly route to Auckland than we had planned, which gave her an immediate 200 mile advantage over our great circle course further north. We had decided to follow the course between the 40° and 50° parallels sailed by *Sayula* and *Pen Duick VI* during the 1973–4 WRTWR because in that year the yachts going north had experienced much stronger winds than those on the shorter route to the south. It was too early to tell whether we had made the right move or not, and we consoled ourselves with a 260 mile run in truly exhilarating conditions on that sixth day. It had been hard work for the crew, constantly changing and trimming sails, but great fun for those taking their turn at the wheel. Maybe now we would start to catch up, I thought.

But no sooner was *Flyer* back in her old stride when the winds died once more. The only saving grace was that the rest of the fleet suffered too. Just where were these high-latitude gales and rolling seas that I had read so much about?

Rob James made us all laugh on the radio show that evening. Each of the crew members aboard *GB II* had paid £4,000 to come on this race and taste the excitement of the Southern Ocean, but apparently his team, frustrated by the calms that they too were experiencing, had demanded a refund because he couldn't deliver the goods described in the brochure!

The winds eventually returned on the eighth day and brought colder air from further south. *Flyer* was again going fast, though with the wind on the nose we were forced to change from spinnaker to headsails. The problem was that the high pressure system was 500–600 miles more south than usual, revolving anticlockwise with its centre on 45°S latitude. While it gave us light headwinds on our more northerly course (around 40°S), the wind was running in the opposite direction further south, to give *Kings Legend* and the crew of *GB II* their money's worth in downwind sailing.

It wasn't until the eleventh day that *Flyer* really broke free from those headwinds (around 45°S), and the mood aboard was by now very depressed. This wasn't helped by the news over the radio that evening that *Kings Legend* was still romping away, eating up 250 miles a day, while we could barely manage 200. Certainly, I wondered if we could ever catch up that amount again, and the prospects looked very grim.

We were now in the midst of the Roaring Forties, yet the seas remained calm – just like the North Sea on a quiet summer's day. The only

difference was that it was rainy and very much colder in these latitudes. I have always felt the cold badly and at the time I wrote on my memo pad 'warm boots required for the Third Leg', which was an understatement. In fact, it was so cold at one point that despite the Webasto diesel heating system (run for an hour at the watch changes) and the heat from the engine, we could never keep warm. Though no-one suffered from frostbite, my feet got so cold that even hot water bottles in my sleeping bag could not thaw them out and I lost all feeling in my toes for two months or more afterwards. However, though cold, the temperature was the only advantage of staying north at this time, for we knew that it would be much colder still where *Kings Legend* was. The trouble was that we were now one of the few boats facing flat calms in the Roaring Forties and we hadn't seen the end of them yet.

On the twelfth day *Kings Legend* was over 340 miles ahead – almost a two day lead, which could have taken us the rest of the race back to Portsmouth

Following the fleet a week later across the Southern Ocean, *Gauloises* experienced none of the calms that beset *Flyer* during the early part of the leg.

to whittle away. It was all very depressing having to face these unusual headwinds while the rest of the fleet ran away under spinnakers. Our bad position was really brought home when *Disque d'Or* passed us on the southerly route and the much smaller *Adventure* and *Traité de Rome* drew level. We were tail-end Charlies now, with one option left: accept that we were behind and run south to join the rest of the fleet. In being overly apprehensive about the conditions in the southern latitudes we were losing out on the favourable winds this year.

That decision proved to be a turning point in the race. Soon afterwards the winds increased to forty knots or more and *Flyer* came alive at last, surfing down the waves at 16 knots plus to give us our first real taste of the Southern Ocean at its best. As each wave picked the boat up by the stern it was as if a giant hand would thrust us forward. She would start to hum like an electric train, vibrations running from stem to stern, bow wave growing higher and higher until all noise was drowned by water and spray.

We just hung on and held our breath, it was like riding a roller coaster down a vertical track. It takes great nerve and skill to keep a boat sailing fast in these conditions; the temptation was always to reduce sail, for once *Flyer* was surfing down the crest of a wave the slightest lapse in concentration would have the boat roll over into a vicious broach, and conceivably could be pinned down on her side at the mercy of the next roller to break over and swamp her.

I had come to the conclusion that we had to attack the ocean rather than wait for the worst to pass if we were to stand any chance of catching up with *Kings Legend*. We just couldn't combine total safety and speed, and either we played safe or went fast to win.

At last the Forties had begun to roar, but far from scaring us, once we had taken this approach the wild conditions brought fresh purpose to our task. As we surfed down each wave an excited call went up: '*Flyer* Go . . . Go . . . Go . . .' and we thumped fists on the deck to will her on.

However, while the winds may have been good, visibility was poor, and without a sun or star sight for three days Jerry was worried about the Kerguellen Islands, a group of shark-toothed rocks that stuck high out of the ocean in latitude 48° 30′S somewhere ahead. It is ironic that when we had the whole of the ocean to sail in we had to tack away to the north to avoid this blot on the chart. The ELAC echosounder showed the bottom rising sharply, and there was a confused, irregular swell, but poor visibility cut out all chance of sighting them unless they were directly in our path. It was certainly an unnerving experience and all eyes kept a sharp watch on deck. The depth meter, which had already proved to be of value in navigation because of its great range, eventually dropped sharply from 130 to over 200 metres to bring relief all round, for it meant we were in the clear at last and back in deep water, without having once sighted the rocks.

We now found that our position in the fleet had improved at last. Indeed we had caught up a little on *Kings Legend*, now only 300 miles ahead. Our gradual move to the south had been right, and to celebrate this first change of luck we had a shot of whisky in the coffee. Morale was given a healthy boost. Chris, always an attraction for birds – whatever variety – befriended a young thing with webbed feet that had flown into the sails and stunned itself. Our guess was that it had come from the Kerguellens, and it followed him around the boat for a full twenty-four hours before flying on again.

In the meantime, *Flyer* pressed on relentlessly, carrying as much sail as she dared, surfing down one wave and crashing head-first into the next. The crew worked themselves to a standstill, first grinding in the sheets on the big winches then letting them out again. The boat creamed on hour after hour, broaching, rolling, shaking and shuddering, spray flying in every direction. Broaches became commonplace, deflecting our progress, sometimes five or six times in an hour, but with every one she would slowly stagger back to her feet and shake herself down like a wet dog, the sails would fill with a noise like the boom from a cannon, the mast vibrated like a reed, and we would be flying on again.

There is nothing to quite compare with Southern Ocean racing. Demanding as it may have been on both crew and equipment, it was a fantastic experience nevertheless. Sails took the hardest hammering of all. On one broach the wire spinnaker sheet tore its way right through the batten pocket on the main, cringles pulled out, and material tore.

But the fight went on. There were 300 miles between us and *Kings Legend* and somehow we had to catch up. At times there was no respite for days on end. The cold was intense, water near freezing, weather wet and miserable, and after every four-hour watch we all just fell in our bunks exhausted.

In these conditions I was always worried that something might break under the enormous strains, and we made daily checks on all rigging and equipment. Chafe was our biggest problem on board. The strains destroyed halyards in days, rather than weeks. Even wire guys could last less than twelve hours; the splices or serving needed regular renewal, and the guys were made overlong so they could be shortened with new splices.

This is what chafe does to the afterguys. They had to be changed every four hours until the Barient pole end fittings were changed for Sparcraft.

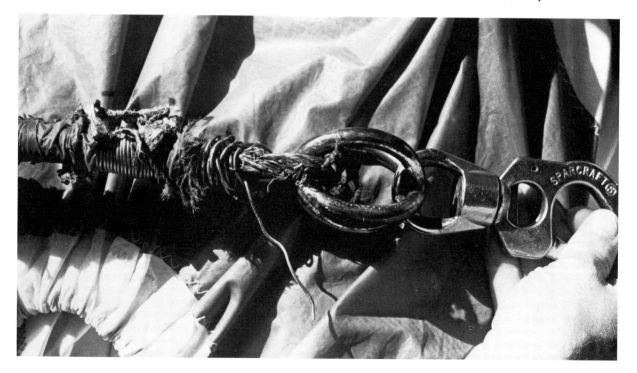

The seventeenth day was marked by a sharply rising barometer and winds that increased all the time. The Forties were really roaring now. One broach saw Ari flung across the deck to leave him helpless in the scuppers, but thank God his lifeline held. It may well have saved his life, for the next wave to crash down would surely have washed him away. Conditions then were so hard that both boat and crew were being tested to the limit. The long-established and standardized routines for sail handling paid off here, where the extreme cold, bulky layers of clothing and rough motion could increase the chances of foulups: crew carried out their jobs without having to listen for shouted orders or advice, and the gear was set up and left in the same way each time.

Our nagging doubts about the chances of something breaking eventually materialized at night, while Chris was on the helm fighting hard to keep the boat on an even course through those high seas. He suddenly lost all feeling on the wheel. Thinking that we had lost the rudder, he sounded the emergency horn to call me up from my bunk. 'We've lost the rudder,' he shouted, and thoughts of an early retirement from this race flashed into my mind. When I opened the aft hatch and saw the steering cable loose around the quadrant and obviously broken, it was a tremendous relief.

Jerry grabbed the emergency tiller and jammed it on the rudder post, Aedgard led his watch to pull down the spinnaker, and Hugh scrambled from his bunk and rushed back aft to make repairs. It was no easy job, for

The spinnaker sheets are led through heavy-duty blocks used on American Twelve Metres. The after one always had a spare sheet rove as spinnaker sheets had to be changed every twenty-four hours.

Spinnaker afterguy, showing the 'doughnut' which, when winched tight against the pole end fitting, helped to reduce chafe.

while *Flyer* bucked and yawed, again on course downwind, nothing was steady. Fingers slipped on the freezing steel, but Hugh knew every inch of the boat. He had the spare cable and tools ready in minutes and within half an hour had wriggled back out, the job completed. His time with Huisman had paid off.

On the nineteenth day *KL* reported a crack in her fibreglass skeg which opened and closed when pressure built up on the rudder as she surged down the waves. It was certainly bad news for them and I hoped, like they did, that it wouldn't develop into a more serious leak. She was now 267 miles ahead, but even if her crew slowed down to relieve the stress it was still going to be a hard fight to catch up with her.

We were now in sight of icebergs; it was bitterly cold and one could stay at the helm for no longer than a half hour spell. But I spared a thought for the crew aboard *Debenhams*, nearly 400 miles further south, who had reported that they were now working their way through pack ice and sighting bergs.

So near to the magnetic South Pole, her crew had been led off course 91 miles to the south by the compass needle, which wanted to point almost directly downwards. Though further north, we too suffered from sluggish compasses which made it extremely difficult to steer. As *Flyer* bore away down a wave, the compass would take so long to react that it would still be following round when the bow was headed up again at the bottom of the trough. It became almost impossible to steer on the compass and we could better judge our direction from the wind and waves.

Soon after this leg had started, I promised to break into the beer and Scotch rations if we managed a run of more than 280 miles in a day – an average of just over $11\frac{1}{2}$ knots, and 2 knots greater than our theoretical top speed. Conditions had begun to harden the next day to set us reaching these great seas with winds abeam – *Flyer*'s favourite point of sailing. She leapt ahead, leeward rail deep, with water thrown in all directions. It was in these conditions, when the boat would surf down the waves at 16 knots or more, that she might just manage to achieve my goal. Anyway, the thought of a Scotch urged us all to get the most out of her.

Communications, like the weather, were now usually very poor (perhaps due to the Aurora Australis, which we often saw) but we had heard above the static that *Kings Legend* was now okay for the time being; the rudder was not wrenching the crack open further, and her pumps were able to cope with the leak. The distance between us had dropped to 207 miles. By contrast, *Traité de Rome* was now 204 miles astern, so we had made ground on everyone. At last, on this twentieth day, events seemed to be running our way.

Meanwhile, *Flyer* surged on and at times more than half her hull would lie suspended in empty air as she surfed down some of those huge rollers. The cloud and snow showers that had come with the gale blotted out all chance of a sun or star sight and for three days Jerry had to calculate our positions by dead reckoning from the speedo and log and the sluggish compasses. However, a great cheer went up when he estimated that *Flyer* had covered 281 miles in one day. It was quite possible for we had been surfing down those rollers at incredible speeds, and the Scotch bottle was brought out immediately.

Unfortunately, no sooner had we all downed our reward when a ray of sunshine broke through the murk. Alas, the new sight left us twenty miles to the northwest of our DR position, so we hadn't quite completed those 281 miles. 'But the whisky was good', Jerry wrote in the log, and I was well pleased with our performance, for *Flyer* was back with a fighting chance now.

During the next radio show we heard that *KL*'s crew were not happy with the leak and had decided to set a course close to Hobart just in case the trouble got worse. Apart from narrowing their lead to 195 miles, we also learned that we were now pulling up on the rest of the fleet and had gained another thirty-five miles on *Traité de Rome*.

While the position reports were being made, Robin Knox-Johnston told us that they had lost a man overboard from *Condor*. The spinnaker sheet had suddenly pulled taut when the sail filled, catching Bill Abram and flicking him over the lifelines while the yacht sailed on at ten knots. Now, *Condor*'s man-overboard drill was similar to ours, but I found out in Auckland later that the helmsman had rounded up before the spinnaker was fully taken down, and it had promptly twisted itself around the rigging. More vital

A view from the helm with 14 knots showing on the top dial.

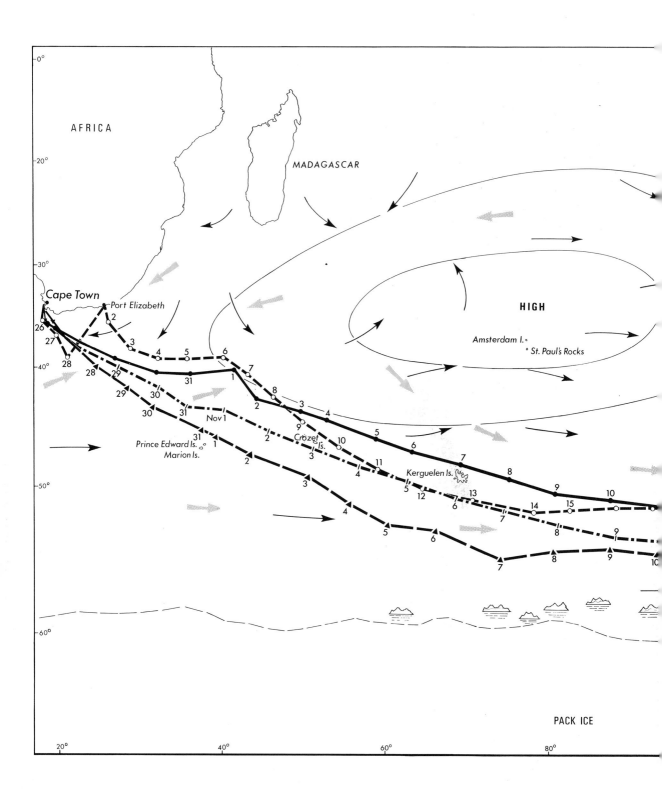

AFRICA

MADAGASCAR

Cape Town
Port Elizabeth

HIGH

Amsterdam I.
St. Paul's Rocks

Prince Edward Is.
Marion Is.

Crozet Is.

Kerguelen Is.

Nov 1

PACK ICE

0°

20°

30°

40°

50°

60°

20°     40°     60°     80°

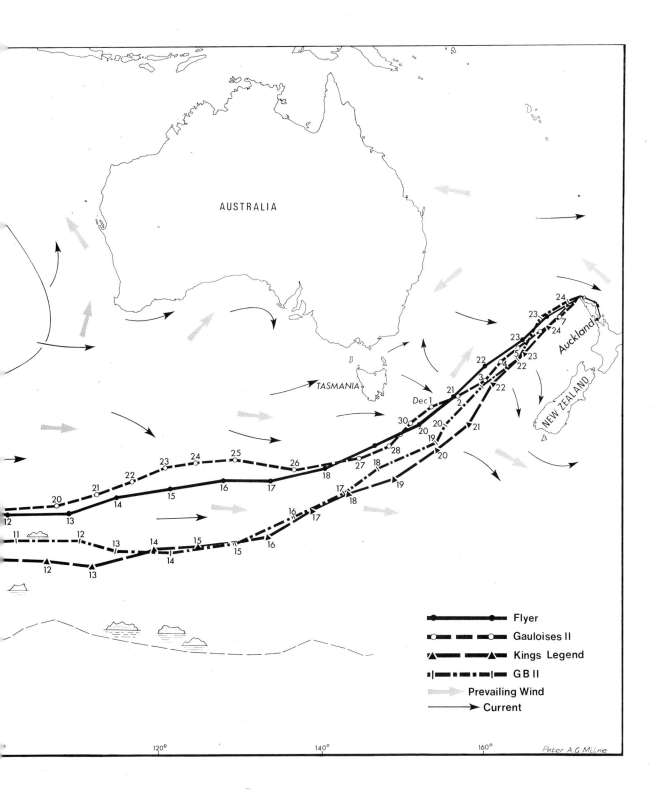

AUSTRALIA

TASMANIA

NEW ZEALAND

Auckland

Dec 1

| | Flyer |
| | Gauloises II |
| | Kings Legend |
| | GB II |
| | Prevailing Wind |
| | Current |

Peter A.G. Milne

120°          140°          160°

minutes were lost when it was found that the folding propeller had jammed shut. Those delays could have been fatal in the colder water still further south, but the crew had been able to throw a lifebuoy to the man immediately after he went over, and were helped to spot his position later from the flock of birds that had been following their wake. Though none attacked him, these graceful creatures continued to swoop down over him inquisitively, thinking he might be food. Bill was a very lucky man and was picked up within ten minutes, very cold but otherwise unharmed.

That same day the other big boat in this race also ran into trouble. One of the men aboard *GB II* was caught up in a loop in the spinnaker afterguy which tightened around him, crushing his waist. The rope (fortunately not wire) had to be cut, and the spinnaker was lost overboard, before he was freed, and he lay below for several days seriously injured. The incident, in which Rob James was also slightly injured, brought home the risks involved in such racing, especially on the bigger boats with their tremendously powerful sails. It was also a blow to morale aboard *GB II*, which was reflected in a sharp drop in boat speed over the next few days.

Our main troubles were torn sails. The head of one spinnaker was blown out completely, the material torn to ribbons, and even Adrian could do nothing with it. Over about 35 knots apparent wind it was more or less a matter of time until heavy spinnakers or flankers (2.2 oz cloth) would go, and of course no-one could know what the weight of wind would be in the squalls. There was no letup: we had to push *Flyer* as hard as possible irrespective of broaches and ruined sails. It was the only way if we were to have any chance to make up the ground lost at the beginning of this leg. These tactics certainly brought results, for in the past seven days we had covered 1,788 miles at an average speed of 10.6 knots – quite impressive when the designers had said *Flyer*'s theoretical hull speed was only 9.6 knots. So far we had run a total of 4,553 miles with another 2,600 to go. The big question was whether we could cover the rest of the distance to Auckland in two weeks: 'The answer was blowing in the wind.'

However, there was no time to stand around and congratulate ourselves, for no sooner had we done our sums when the main boom was snapped in two by the force of water against it when *Flyer* went into another ferocious broach. Luckily the mainsail was not damaged, but it took Aedgard and Hugh ten hours to repair the spar, utilizing a spare section as an internal sleeve and a section of toerail track bolted and riveted on the outside as reinforcement. The wind was so strong at the time that the absence of our mainsail for this period made no difference to speed and *Flyer* continued reaching through the seas at an average 10 knots. This was not the first time our boom had dragged in the water when off the wind, and other yachts also suffered similar damage. To take the strain off the repair, after this the end of

Broken during a broach by the force of water rushing past, the boom took less than ten hours to repair using a spare mast section and part of the toerail.

the boom was always raised with the reefing line in such conditions.

On the twenty-second day *Kings Legend* reported that her leak was not getting worse, thank goodness, and that they had decided to press on as hard as they could – which was not quite such good news. Could we continue to outsail them now, I wondered?

Boxing was the topic at the time with the watch below, who had been reading about a Muhammed Ali fight. This reminded Rod of a story that certainly amused all the 'foreigners' aboard. An English commentator describing the boxers back home as 'our horizontal heavyweights' had so incensed followers of the sport in Britain that he had been sued for libel and brought to justice, even though his comments might have had some element of truth.

By the twenty-third day at sea the winds had dropped slightly but the swell was as huge as ever, picking *Flyer* up to throw her ahead and making it impossible to keep a steady course. She would surf down a wave, spray climbing halfway up to the spreaders, broach, shake herself free, and then surge down the next. It was just amazing what both boat and crew could stand up to.

The next day, though, we learned that *Flyer* had lost a little ground to *Kings Legend*, now five miles further ahead, but as *Traité de Rome* was now 330 miles astern we consoled ourselves that the boys on *KL* had probably enjoyed better winds. There was now less than 1,900 miles left to catch her in, and if the winds held strong enough we could complete the leg in ten days. What we needed was wind, wind, and more wind!

In answer, however, the gods left us totally becalmed for the night, though next morning the winds came back hard, gusting to fifty knots and more. We set the heavy reaching spinnaker, put three reefs in the main and held on tight. Unfortunately, it didn't last long. The winds backed 15° in five minutes, than dropped to a force 3–4, and what worried me most was the thought of those other boats forging on ahead.

But they didn't. From the radio show that night we heard that *GB II* had also had a very slow twenty-four hours, while we gained another fifty miles on *Traité de Rome*, and *Kings Legend* had dropped right back to within 137 miles. She was now hampered by loose rudder fittings, to add to her troubles, which made it more difficult to steer through heavy seas. I knew that *Flyer's* position on handicap was beginning to look up at last. On Jerry's reckoning we were now fourth on this leg and second overall in the race, which was much better than we had been ten days before.

The next day Bruce reported problems with the engine. During the daily run to charge batteries and keep the deepfreeze operating, it had suddenly died. The problem was traced to a fault in the fuel pipe, which we had suspected for some time since air had leaked mysteriously into the injectors on other occasions. The only answer was to bypass the pipe completely with a makeshift header tank made up from a hastily adapted plastic water can. This was set up above the engine to act as a gravity feed and for the rest of the leg it was topped up each day from the diesel tank.

Our time at sea in this cold, uncomfortable ocean had begun to tell. Skin, especially on the hands, had become cracked, hard and chapped, and *Flyer* herself was beginning to look the worse for wear – broken main boom, missing toerail track, bent stanchions and scratched hull paintwork. The bent stanchions had been caused by the low-cut genoas shipping water in the foot, which pushed them outwards as much as 30°; the same strain also bent the low bulwark. Most of the crew were taking vitamin C pills to keep colds and 'flu at bay, but they had little effect for we all suffered from sniffles and sore throats. Under our boots and oilskins we were wearing layers of clothing to try to keep warm: balaclavas, furry polar suits, long

Adrian Ford, wearing two balaclavas to keep out the penetrating cold.

woollen stockings inside loosely-fitting wetsuit bootees. Gloves were a matter for individual experiment, and in general heavy plastic-coated industrial gloves such as are used by commercial fishermen were worn over woollen or other inner gloves. To keep the water out, we wore unlined and lined oilskin trousers together.

But *Flyer* was rolling on at top speed to Auckland and that was all that mattered. The twenty-sixth day was another good run of 252 miles in 24 hours to narrow *Kings Legend*'s lead by 26 miles and leave another 50 between us and *Traité de Rome*. We also heard that the lead held by *Condor* had dropped to 516 miles, and, somewhat optimistically, I wondered if we could catch up with her too. The sails were now looking very much the worse for wear, and with much better radio reception we were able to get an order through to Hood Sailmakers in Auckland for two new spinnakers.

That day conditions built up again to storm force and every now and then a vicious gust would knock *Flyer* over on her beam ends. She was sailing under the reaching spinnaker and genoa staysail together with a triple-reefed main and double-reefed mizzen, and when the squalls hit she was well overpressed. We did a great deal of spinnaker reaching, and in these conditions found it necessary to use wire guys to keep the pole off the headstay. The wire cut or damaged any sails which it rubbed, and sheets passing under the boom or near the mainsail leech were also sources of serious chafe. This meant extra effort in rigging up ways to prevent contact, and great care in winching the wire to prevent riding turns or slipping. The boat would roll, shudder and zoom through the seas alarmingly, but it was the only way to keep up our speed. We just had to hold on tight, grin and bear it, for if *Flyer* could take it so must we.

For the third night running, there was more good news on the radio show. *Kings Legend*'s lead had now been narrowed to 96 miles – just nine hours ahead at these speeds – and *Traité de Rome* was dropping further astern. We had also taken 26 miles out of the 77 ft *Heath's Condor*, and for the first time in two weeks we heard from *GB II* who was 274 miles ahead. *Flyer*'s handicap position was improving by the hour, and we now knew that if we could continue at this pace there was a chance to recapture the lead.

However, there were always some problems to contend with and our next was a spinnaker halyard block on a masthead crane that disintegrated with a bang. This time we were lucky, for the halyard itself was held by the exit box and internal sheave; if the rope had been cut through by chafe, which could happen very quickly, the boat would have run right over the sail. It gave Ari the chance to get up to his monkey tricks again and he was hoisted up to fit a replacement. The heavier the swell, the more he liked it at the top of the mast and on this occasion he had the time of his life, for the rollers really pounded in.

Chafe-preventing covers over the shrouds and temporary blocks to lead the spinnaker sheet clear of the boom and mainsheet.

In these conditions one has to have an extremely steady hand on the helm to keep *Flyer* on an even keel, for once she starts to roll a broach is inevitable. Steering was far from easy, since you had to judge both wind and waves and set the boat up for any changes well before they affected you. It was during one of these rolling sessions that *Flyer* suffered her worst broach of the voyage. After the first roll, with Bruce on the wheel, Jerry took over but he had no time to clip his lifeline on before a sudden squall hit us, rolling *Flyer* again and throwing him into the scuppers. The boat was knocked right on her beam ends; water poured down the Dorade box to wash Aedgard from his bunk, and plates, cutlery, sailbags and personal belongings were scattered everywhere below. It was all quite a mess, but we quickly had *Flyer* under control again and sailing on at speed.

We waited eagerly for the radio chat show every twenty-four hours. Sometimes, when we had a good day's run to report, those minutes waiting felt more like hours and on that day it was certainly no different. But eventually the positions came through and it was calculated that we had taken another twenty-six miles out of *KL* and that both *Adventure* and *Traité de Rome* were running neck-and-neck 548 miles back. We also heard that *Disque d'Or* was 180 miles astern, and that we had even gained again on *Condor*, now just 435 miles ahead. At last we had really begun to pull back effectively, and everything was going well for us. During the past week *Flyer* had run 1,717 miles and the total distance sailed so far had been 6,270 miles: an average of 9.2 knots. There was 900 miles to go and we just had to hope that the weather would hold to the finish. By this time well into the Tasman Sea with the water so much warmer, we could wash ourselves in sea water again after three weeks.

Previously, in Cape Town, I had been warned that New Zealand import controls banned yachts from bringing in any foodstuffs, and with our deepfreeze still well stocked I decided it was better to eat steak for breakfast, lunch and dinner than have to ditch it all overboard later. For the last week at sea we all lived like lords and even broke into the beer rations, lest these also were covered by the same regulations. It was all good for morale, and the closeness of the racing kept our competitive drive up while the relentless pursuit continued. *Kings Legend*'s lead dropped from 74 miles one day to 45 miles the next.

Auckland loomed up over the horizon on the thirty-third day, and while we knew that both *Condor* and *GB II* had finished the previous day, *Kings Legend* kept quiet about her position. There had been only two hours separating us after the leg to Cape Town: had we narrowed her lead to within that time?

There was just no way of knowing, and suspense grew as the wind started to drop nearer the land. Would it hold to the finish? Had we

A dawn meeting at the finish line. *Kings Legend* was there to greet us having come in just an hour and fifteen minutes ahead.

sailed hard enough? Why did it take us so long deciding to go south? All these thoughts ran through my mind as we crept on towards the gun. But the winds did hold – just – and we crossed the line on the very last of the night breeze to see *Kings Legend* waiting to greet us. She had finished one hour and fifteen minutes ahead, to leave us with an overall lead on handicap of just forty-six minutes – an incredibly small gap after racing halfway round the world.

*33 Export*, the 56-footer driven by a keen French crew under Alain Gabbay, eventually won this leg on handicap and was followed by *Traité de Rome*. *Kings Legend* was third, with *Flyer* fourth; the first boats to arrive, *Condor* and *GB II*, dropped to eighth and ninth respectively, again unable to hold their time against the smaller, more efficient yachts. We had completed this second part of the race (logged distance of 7,118 miles) at an average speed of 9.3 knots in 32 days 5 hours and 3 minutes, in conditions that no-one will ever forget.

The list of jobs to be completed before the start of the third leg to Rio (see Appendix) was not as large as it had been in Cape Town. A 3 inch crack in the skeg plating, about halfway down, was found and welded, and new Teflon rudder bushes were made by a local engineering shop to replace the originals, which had begun to wear. A new boom was supplied by an Auckland mast maker, a hydraulic boom vang leak fixed, and the mizzen vang overhauled, and all halyards and sheets were replaced from the supplies sent out to us by Huisman. As at Cape Town, his crate had been waiting for us at the quayside when we finished.

With all this work going on one could very easily forget which items had been removed. It happened to Jerry one evening after a few jars of beer ashore. Talking to Bruce back on board, he instinctively leant back on the lifeline round the deck and promptly fell overboard: rather foolishly, it had been removed ready for a replacement to be fitted the next day. Simon Willis, watch leader and *Flyer*'s main taskmaster on the Transatlantic Race, now headed the Hood service loft in Auckland and he and Adrian set about to repair and replace the many chafed and torn remnants of our sail wardrobe. The spare main and pole were to be left off, but some spinnakers and reaching sails were replaced or supplemented with heavier versions.

Once work was completed, there was time off to enjoy ourselves. Most set off to explore New Zealand while I flew to Los Angeles for ten days to meet my wife Inger and to discuss business with my associates. I had done precious little of this kind of work for the last six months! It was an enjoyable break and great fun to be with Inger again, whom I hadn't seen since we had left Portsmouth.

On the long flight back afterwards I met John Kilroy, son and heir to Jim Kilroy of Kilroy Industries and the owner of the beautiful S&S designed

*Disque d'Or* and *Kings Legend*, hauled out at Auckland for similar skeg repairs. The difference in stern shapes between the two Swans is readily apparent; *KL*'s stern has been extended in an effort to reduce her tendency to 'squat' in the water.

*Flyer* gets a scrub and new paint.

*Gauloises II* out of the water again for a thorough check, particularly of her rudder.

maxi-rater *Kialoa*. She had been in Auckland undergoing major hull surgery prior to competing in the Southern Cross Series in Australia, where John Kilroy was now bound. *Kialoa* had already been across the Southern Ocean twice in sailing from one race series to another, and I asked why his father never competed in events like the Round the World Race.

'Well, the Whitbread Race boats pose no real competition for either our boat or crew,' was the brash retort, and after such a slap in the face I challenged him there and then to compete against us in any long ocean race – but he made no reply. I read in the newspapers a few days later that *Kialoa* had just had a collision with her arch rival *Windward Passage* in one of the races off Sydney Heads, and that young Kilroy had fallen over the side. It was a story that brought broad smiles to the air hostesses on that flight, who later came down to visit *Flyer* before we set off again. After my challenge to young Kilroy they had had their work cut out controlling his youthful excesses.

My own thought is that *Kialoa*, now with very similar lines to *Flyer*'s underwater shape, is rigged too lightly for this kind of racing. *Flyer* had been tested to the limit on this leg, yet here was a boat with a 72 ft waterline against our 50 ft, with standing and running rigging and equipment no stronger than ours. Her blocks, halyards, spinnaker pole end fittings and spar sections were all comparable to those on *Flyer*, and I was amazed that they weren't all much stronger and heavier. Her skipper, Bruce Kendall, recounting a very fast passage across from America, talked of waves that were higher than their mizzen mast – and when you realize that *Kialoa*'s mizzen is almost as tall as the mainmast on *Flyer*, they must have been some waves! He thought that the crew had driven the boat very fast, but of course they were not racing. If they had been, I think they would have had problems.

While I was away from Auckland Eric Tabarly arrived with his famous *Pen Duick VI*, intending to enter the final two legs to Rio and Portsmouth. This yacht, though put out of the running by breaking two masts in the first WRTWR, had proved to be very fast, and with her Tabarly went on to win the Singlehanded Transatlantic Race, after sailing through the most appalling conditions. However, *Pen Duick*'s entry was soon shrouded in controversy when Leslie Williams issued a protest against the Frenchman. In fact, it was more of a complaint than a protest, for while *Condor* carried an 'exotic material' rating penalty throughout the race for her light carbon fibre reinforced mast, even though it had been replaced halfway through the first leg with a conventional aluminium one, *Pen Duick* suffered no such penalty for her exotic keel. This had been cast from spent uranium, which is much denser than lead but now disallowed because of its high cost and

Eric Tabarly keeping thoughts
to himself on *Pen Duick VI*
while the Race Committee
debated what to do about his
yacht's rating certificate.

restricted availability, for international offshore racing.

The protest committee found that there were no means available under the Race Rules to penalise *Pen Duick VI*, but while checking through the details it was found that the French yacht carried an outdated and therefore invalid IOR rating certificate. With just two days before the start of the third leg there was no time to check whether the French authorities had as claimed issued a valid certificate for her, so it was decided to allow Tabarly to start as a provisional entry while the vexed question of eligibility was resolved.

It was during this stay in Auckland that John and Marie-Christine Ridgway invited me to dinner, and talk centred around the subject of crew management: there had been a growing rebellion on board *Debenhams* against the structure of authority, and even the basic discipline of sailing. I told him that he had asked for trouble by allowing a film team on board who were not committed to the effort involved in racing, yet freely discussing and recording all the crews' grievances behind his back. I made it clear to my crew from the start that all questions and requests for interviews from the press were to be referred to me. The sole exception was Jerry Dijkstra's arrangement to write some technical articles for a Dutch yachting magazine.

# Across the Pacific

Every fifth Aucklander owns a boat and I think each one of those must have been out afloat to see the start of the third leg from Auckland on Boxing Day. The scene was just incredible – thousands of boats weaving plaited wakes around us, honking their horns and shouting farewell, to make it by far the biggest send-off in the race.

Starting on the same line that the One Tonners had used during their World Championship the month before, we were careful this time not to run in early. A recall gun was fired, indicating at least one premature starter, but from where *Flyer* was, well behind the line, we just couldn't tell who, although this didn't stop us from having a great deal of fun calling across to Nick Ratcliffe to suggest that it was *Kings Legend* who had been recalled. Now it is never easy to sail through the lee of a yacht, especially one as well handled as *KL*, but this time we shot past as if they were anchored. There was a great deal of gesticulating aboard while her crew argued among themselves whether they were over the line or not. The answer to their confusion only came once *Flyer* had broken through and we had offered a cheery wave to thank them very much.

In fact, it had been *GB II* who was well over the line, with *33 Export* also across early. Neither answered the gun to turn back and in any other race of this length could probably have expected a twenty-four hour penalty – that was what we hoped, anyway. However, the Committee decided to add just a ten minute penalty to *GB II*'s time and five minutes to *33 Export*, which, though neither knew their penalty until Rio, did not make it worthwhile to turn back: by the time they had gybed round through the massive fleet of spectator craft, twenty minutes could have been lost. Indeed, this is what happened to *Disque d'Or* which lost hours in returning to the line after her crew had thought that they were the culprits. Fortunately, this misunderstanding did not hit her chances too hard, for she caught up with the fleet again the next day when we were held up by calms.

The light breezes continued into the third day and *GB II* was first to be seen slowly overhauling us on the fine reach towards Matakoe Point,

The black-hulled *Pen Duick VI* towers over the many small
spectator boats out to watch the start at Auckland.

though we held our ground during the short-tacking duel to clear the headland. By rights, *GB II*, because of her size, should have been much faster than *Flyer* on all points of sailing, but her sails were now so badly out of shape after the storms and ill-treatment of the second leg, and in need of professional attention, that in light weather at least we could now outsail her boat for boat.

There were 4,400 miles between us and Cape Horn and a further 2,300 miles to Rio, and though it was gratifying to see *GB II* drop away to leeward, it was *Kings Legend*'s position I was more interested in. *GB II* was no longer a threat to our overall position, for in order to beat us on this leg she had to finish more than 4 days, 16 hours ahead of us at Rio, and 14 days, 1 hour ahead to beat us in the overall standings – a tremendous task when you consider that she had only beaten us to the finish on the second leg by less than a day. It was *Kings Legend* that remained *Flyer*'s biggest threat with a mere forty-seven minutes to make up on our time. If her crew had broken away again like they did on the second leg, we could well have lost all chance of winning. *Disque d'Or* was in third place overall, and though carrying a lower handicap than *Flyer* now had to finish 1 day, 17 hours ahead of us to get back into the reckoning at Rio. *Traité de Rome*, with her cosmopolitan crew from the nine EEC countries, lay fourth, and doing much better than I had expected, had to finish within 1 day, 17 hours of us to challenge the overall standings. *Adventure* was the only other yacht in the race that could finish behind us and still take over the overall lead, but only by coming within a mere three hours of us.

Because of their previous disastrous breakages, both *Heath's Condor* and *Gauloises* were now out of the hunt, unless something extraordinary happened; *Flyer* now had an eighteen day advantage over *Condor* and more than seven days over the French yacht.

Although *Pen Duick* and *Condor* sailed away over the horizon on the fourth day, the light winds kept *GB II* three miles abeam and her silhouette acted as a goad to keep *Flyer* driving as fast as possible. In Auckland we had shed more than a ton of unwanted sails and equipment from *Flyer* and shifted the remaining stores to the centre in an effort to lighten her stern and reduce drag. This had certainly improved performance, and our position alongside *GB II*, with *Kings Legend* unable to overtake, vindicated all that hard work at the quayside.

Those light winds persisted for a frustrating seven days, although at times we were able to catch right up with *Pen Duick* and *Condor* while they lay becalmed. It was a week of constant sail-changing and trimming, and although it was not strenuous work we all suffered badly from tiredness. It also became increasingly difficult to concentrate throughout a four-hour watch and harder still to stay awake when one's duties were over. The symptoms kept us guessing for some time, until I wondered if it might be a lack of salt. After issuing tablets, and taking some myself, there was a miraculous recovery among the crew, and although he could not explain why, the Doc liked the cure.

The weather eventually changed in time for the New Year and as we drank champagne to celebrate, sang songs and sent flares high into the sky, the night glow slowly grew blacker, dark clouds rolled across and rain began to fall. It was a torrential downpour but with it came wind – a force 4 to start with that slowly built up into a gale right on the nose that gave our small jibs their first airing during the race. *Flyer* leapt at the waves, well heeled over with the sheets wound in hard, but however uncomfortable the motion might have been it was a welcome change from the fickle conditions that prevailed during the previous week. We set a cutter rig, which, though not as efficient as a single genoa, offered a quick and simple way to reduce sail in the squally conditions, since the jib could be lowered quickly whenever the boat was overpressed.

That night was certainly a wet and wild one with seas building up into an enormous swell, but *Flyer* sailed on attacking each one in turn, winning through in a plume of spray. Life was difficult on board, both above and below decks, when the world was canted at 30° like this, but news that the tables were now turned on *Kings Legend* was a real fillip to morale. She had fallen 46 miles astern and *Traité de Rome* was a further 100 miles back. Our prospects were looking good.

The bigger yachts, however, had at last found their legs and moved ahead faster in the stronger conditions. *GB II* and *Pen Duick*, further to the north and enjoying a more favourable beam wind, had gained 92 miles, though *Condor* was still very close. Les Williams was still experiencing serious troubles with the rig, which had not been so apparent on the downwind second leg. For windward work *Condor*'s metal replacement mast was too 'soft', bending and twisting alarmingly as she pounded through the waves, and scared of being dismasted a second time, he did not dare to overload the spar.

But the constant and monotonous pounding through the seas was having its effect on *Flyer* too. One wire strand in the aft lower shroud snapped under the pressure, but fortunately Jerry spotted the damage during the daily check before it got worse. We carried spare wire aboard for just such an eventuality and Aedgard prepared a length with a Norseman terminal on one end, ready to replace the shroud once we tacked to transfer the strains across to the opposite side of the rig.

Some of the waves were enormous during that gale, and though *Flyer* was not unduly troubled, *33 Export* almost came to grief. She was hit from ahead by a vertical wall of water that broke right over the deck, throwing

Closehauled and reefed well down. On *Flyer* the reefing system is very simple with no special fittings. The reefing lines are tied around the boom and run through the leech cringles, over sheaves in the boom end, and through the spar to a special winch near the mast.

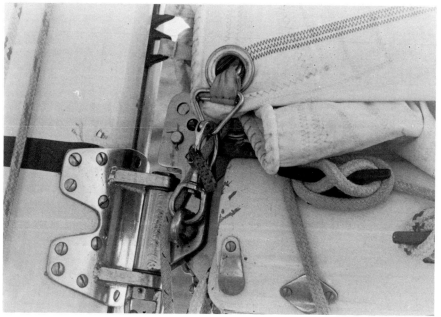

Reefing gear on the main boom consisted of Sparcraft snap shackles and stoppers to change over the reefing lines (not shown).

the boat on its side. The tool chest was emptied; spanners, files, rasps and screwdrivers stuck themselves into the gallery ceiling; tins of food were scattered everywhere; charts, notebooks and barometer fell from the chart table straight into the WC; retaining straps holding the batteries snapped and the boxes smashed the saloon floor, with one spinning into the lee bunk to land on Philippe Schaff who was injured in the stomach. The boat finished up in a terrible mess, and from the trajectory of displaced tools it was estimated that she had rolled more than 140° from the vertical. However, her crew soon pumped out the water that had flooded below and continued sailing to cover 197 miles in the day: quite an achievement.

On the eleventh day the winds finally dropped with the sun making a welcome reappearance to allow Jerry to take his first noon sight for several days. Unfortunately, he found that *Flyer* had travelled 20 miles less than estimated, though we still gained on *Kings Legend* who was now a full 65 miles astern. That error was due to the absence of any westerly current, which normally runs in this part of the world at ten to twelve miles a day. The strong adverse winds had held it back.

That same day *Adventure* relayed a message from Race Control that *Pen Duick VI* did not have a valid IOR rating certificate and was therefore ineligible to compete in the race. Though Tabarly's radio man just uttered a startled 'Oh!' when he received the decision, and closed down transmission, it proved to be the main talking point on the radio net, and an indignant John Ridgway suggested that a protest telegram be sent to the Race Committee demanding a full explanation. Clare Francis agreed, and asked other yachts what they thought. *Flyer* was the only yacht to go against the motion and we asked for our name to be deleted from the telegram, pointing out that it was the Committee who ran this race, not the competitors.

In fact, it made no difference to us whether *Pen Duick* raced or not because she was only competing in half the event and could not challenge our overall position. Rules are needed to run a race like this, just as they are needed in life, and if a competitor cannot measure up to them I felt he should not have entered. Tabarly knew full well before he even sailed to Auckland that *Pen Duick* did not have a valid certificate. Her uranium keel had just precluded her from being eligible for the Trans-Pac Race, but he had entered this event all the same, perhaps trusting that no-one would raise a query.

Clare, sounding hurt over the radio, went back to the other yachts, saying that since *Flyer* would not play ball maybe they should all think the matter over a little longer before sending the telegram. Later, more were to agree with my point of view. Tabarly himself took the decision philosophically enough and continued to Rio without letting up the pace.

Later, the Committee encouraged him to continue racing with the fleet on the fourth leg to Portsmouth, and although he refused to accept a boat for boat bet against *Flyer* he took on a wager against Robin Knox-Johnston and *Condor* for two crates of champagne.

On the thirteenth day the winds returned to moderate force at last and *Flyer* continued on her favourite point of sailing to reach through the seas at high speed averaging 9.8 knots during the day in force 3 conditions. While the sailing might have been easier, there were some other worries. Rob James reported that *GB II* had spotted three icebergs, and Clare Francis said that *ADC* had also spotted some. It was a timely warning and from then on we kept a better twenty-four hour lookout for these white monsters. Our main worry was that *Flyer* might run one down at night, or hit a growler – a chip off one of the giant icebergs – either of which could do serious damage to the hull.

We also had news over the radio that both *Japy-Hermes* and *Gauloises* had blown out spinnakers, which warned us that a further weather front was coming across. Sure enough, the next day the weather changed. Dark clouds rolled away to produce a clear blue sky and warm sun – a perfect skating day back in Holland, I noted in my own log. But with those beautiful conditions came another gale, and quickly changing down from heavy spinnakers to genoas, we cracked in sheets and held on. *Flyer* surged ahead just like she had on the second leg, rolling, crashing and pounding through waves to run an exhilarating 230 miles in the day.

In these two weeks we had now covered 2,766 miles at an average speed of 8.2 knots, which was not bad in view of the calms experienced during the first three days. We now reckoned it would be another eight days before we could see the Horn, one of the important reasons why most of us had decided to enter this race in the first instance. Rounding the Horn is the ultimate in every sailor's dream. Would it match up to the horror stories of the past or give us a fair passage through, I wondered at the time.

Surprisingly, *Kings Legend* had not been on the air for two days, which was worrying because I didn't expect them to play games with us in this part of the ocean. Their silence really brought home the fact that if anything ever went wrong there was just no-one out here to help us. It was one of the risks we all had to accept on this adventure and I just hoped they were okay. Meanwhile, *GB II* continued to romp ahead and was now 130 miles up on *Condor*, who continued with so little sail up that she could barely outpace us each day. Indeed, we reckoned at the time that she must have been just over the horizon, no more than ten miles ahead.

Although wet and cold, the temperatures were not nearly as low as those experienced on the second leg and so far we had not even sighted an iceberg, even though most of the other yachts had by now had some close encounters. Sailing through fog, *Traité de Rome* came up to a giant iceberg no more than 200 metres straight ahead and was forced to make an all-standing gybe to avoid it. It was certainly a frightening experience, and the story kept eyes well peeled aboard *Flyer*.

We also ran into fog patches, and as so often happens when visibility is reduced to little more than a boat length, the winds died away as well to leave us totally becalmed. We sat for a whole day with *Flyer* barely able to make any headway as the eye of a low-pressure system crossed overhead. It was a very frustrating time, made worse with news that 30-knot westerlies had helped *Pen Duick* to stride 160 miles ahead and allowed *Traité de Rome* to gain 63 miles on us and *Tielsa* 70. Only *Condor* and *GB II* suffered from the same conditions, and for the three of us it was a disastrous 24 hours.

Swinging in the breeze: repair work aboard *Kings Legend*.

To make matters worse, we also had an influenza bug aboard which affected everyone and Doc was called into action for the first time. I was one of the worst hit, suffering with a long attack of bronchitis which lasted for ten days, and during one night suffered from a very high fever and violent chest pains whenever I coughed. It was certainly an unpleasant time for us all, but the way to recovery was no doubt helped by the sudden appearance of Playgirl of the Month pinned up in the cabin. Deborah Jensen was her name – a lovely girl!

The seventeenth night was easily the wettest of the race, for with winds gusting force 6–7 it drove the rain right at us to sting eyes and skin unmercifully and make it quite miserable for those working on deck. The boat drove on relentlessly, crashing through the seas without a worry – or so we thought. The next morning when the gale had died out, Jerry found that one side of the bow had been badly dented. We couldn't have hit anything without the noise vibrating through *Flyer* as if she were a hollow drum, and there was no leak. Normally the slightest sounds are heard throughout the ship, but nothing untoward was recorded that night. Our only conclusion was that the damage must have been caused during the gale, when the boat fell off a wave into the trough below. The power of the sea is sometimes almost unbelievable.

The light winds that prevailed during the day were no more than a lull before the next storm that raged through the following night. We changed down but were caught out by a sudden squall of such ferocity that it tore the heavy reaching spinnaker to ribbons, pulling the cloth clear off the leech tapes, beyond repair. We had to pull the remnants down and send a cable to Hood ordering a replacement for the last leg. But our sail worries were minor compared to the anxiety I felt for those guys aboard *Kings Legend*, since now no-one had heard from them for five days. I was very anxious about their safety, but there was just nothing we could do – a search would have been futile in this vast ocean – and I could only report the fact to Race Control and hope to hear from them soon.

Despite the gale that night, *Flyer* continued to lose out on the rest of the fleet and for the third time on this leg found that the leading boats, both to the south and north of us, had gained from more favourable conditions. *Traité de Rome* was then only 253 miles astern, *Gauloises* was posing a real threat to us on this leg 158 miles back, and *GB II* was 137 miles ahead. We were badly in need of the same following winds that they enjoyed. Our prayers were eventually answered the next day, but not before Jerry badly injured himself after slipping in the cockpit. He landed awkwardly on his wrist while trying to step from one side to the other, straining it so badly that it was impossible for him to use his hand for another ten days. It couldn't have happened at a worse time for the seas had started to build up again for what was obviously going to be another dose of strong winds.

That little bit of forecasting proved to be the biggest understatement of the race, for within hours the winds were blowing up to 70 knots – hurricane force. We hurriedly took the mizzen down, but no sooner had that been furled than the 2.6 oz flanker blew out. Minutes later, the foot tape tore off the blast reacher and everyone held on for dear life, lifelines clipped to the stoutest parts of the boat. We put two slab reefs into the mainsail and set the large jib poled out on the opposite side with the spinnaker pole. It was the first time we had not had a spinnaker up when the wind was astern during this race, but conditions were so bad that I didn't dare try any more canvas. *Flyer* leapt ahead, quivering from stem to stern as she surfed down those massive rollers, some reaching 40 feet above us. She rolled and pitched, but was steady on course and easy to steer. Each time her decks slowly rose up above the boiling foam, the sails would give a shake, and we hurtled on towards the Horn.

While riding the crest of one big wave soon after dawn, we spotted our first iceberg a mile away. It was small compared to some pictures I had seen but was nevertheless an awe-inspiring sight, half-hidden by rollers with seas breaking right across. This was how I had envisaged the Southern Ocean.

Approaching the halfway stage on the nineteenth day, we eventually picked up a faint call from *Kings Legend*. Their voices were quite a relief and the first anyone had heard from them for more than thirteen days. Though signals were very weak, we could just make out that everything was okay but didn't pick up their position. Later in Rio, I learned that water had gushed up through an open toilet valve during one violent broach, which washed out their radio.

The gale eventually died down to a force 3 once more, but blowing over

One of the few occasions in the Southern Ocean when wind conditions were so strong that we were forced to take down the spinnaker and run under twin headsails.

our quarter; *Flyer* continued at a cracking pace – 215 miles that day compared to the 246 miles achieved during the height of the storm. However, both *GB II* and *Condor* gained 50 miles on us, their longer length giving them the advantage in these big seas, although we in turn also increased our lead on the smaller boats. *Traité de Rome*, for instance, was then 380 miles astern and much less of a threat. For the past week we had been having problems with the spinnaker pole end fittings, which were now a loose fit and had a tendency to open at the most inappropriate moments. Aedgard had the job of sorting out the repairs and managed to get the starboard pole working properly again, but its opposite number on the port side remained suspect for the rest of this leg. Another problem was the old one of continuous chafe between sails, halyards and equipment. The halyard exit sheaves at the top of the mast were wearing excessively, and to reduce chafe on the spinnaker halyards, especially in strong winds, Aedgard eventually had to lead one rope through a block outside the mast and not down its centre.

Some of the sailbags were permanently fitted around the tack strop of the sail they contained. Just beyond the bag can be seen the protective disc or 'doughnut' on a spare afterguy.

Fortunately we still had a good radio connection with Wellington, NZ and apart from reporting the problems aboard *Kings Legend*, cabled Hood to make up more spinnakers to replace those ruined in the last storm. Chris, who had been suffering from a problem no tablets could cure – lovesickness – sent a cable to the apple of his eye in Auckland. It read, '800 MILES TO CAPE HORN. THIRD BOAT AT PRESENT. EVERYTHING GREAT ON BOARD. MISS YOU. TAKE CARE. LOVE CHRIS.' 'This was the one,' he had kept telling us. 'I am so in love with her.' For a time I wondered if this big man 'with a girl in every port' was suffering badly from the ill-effects of isolation. The malaise continued throughout this leg but fortunately the symptoms quickly disappeared once he had the chance to taste the highlife in Rio.

The winds picked up once more on the twenty-first day to give us a fabulous wild run through the night, *Flyer* surfing throughout. Sails cracked as the wind tore at the cloth and at one time we covered 47 miles in four hours. Unfortunately the fun didn't last for the winds dropped and veered, forcing us to gybe to keep on course. But we weren't doing so badly,

Wet and cold in the Southern Ocean.

having covered 4,213 miles at an average of 8.4 knots. Eric Tabarly was doing better, having taken a more northerly course and avoided the calms that *Flyer* had run into. *Pen Duick* was 370 miles ahead at the time and had she not been disqualified would have been well placed to take both line and handicap honours for this leg, if she continued to forge ahead.

The twenty-fourth day, January 17, was met with overcast sky, squalls and a race against *Condor* to Cape Horn. Les Williams' course had left him with a beat towards this rocky outpost while *Flyer* continued under spinnakers. This was where the Southern Ocean meets the Atlantic, where waters turn from grey-green to brown and winds can build up to hurricane force within hours. Previously I had read that in this region the weather was almost always bad, blowing a full gale most days, a storm the rest, and building up to hurricane force for three days every three months or so. However, there are odd days when the gods smile sweetly on this region, the winds abate, and huge rollers recede from a ferocious forty to sixty feet to mere twenty foot ripples!

In some ways small yachts like *Flyer* have it easier than the square-riggers that used to ply these treacherous waters. With their wide sterns, those ships were continually in danger of being pooped by the huge following seas. The man at the wheel, and there often had to be two or more, were protected by strong iron shelters, as much to prevent them looking aft at the huge seas breaking over as to save them from being washed away. One man was washed from the foredeck of a ship when it dipped its bow into the seas, then, half drowned, he was dumped back onto the poop deck by the next following wave. It was a miraculous escape, for most who fall overboard here are never seen again, but I was told he lived to tell the tale to whoever would listen for at least fifty years afterwards.

As far as conditions for *Flyer*'s rounding were concerned, I was not too sure what I would have preferred. Light winds would lose us valuable time and in some way cheat us of the real experience. This is what had happened to Kees Bruynzeel when he had sailed round many years before; so flat were the seas that he put ashore to have a picnic, but after discussion with his crew turned back to re-round again when the weather had changed – just to say that he had done it properly!

*GB II* had passed through into the Atlantic eighteen hours ahead of us without trouble, but as we sighted the Diego Ramirez Islands at the expected time and distance we sat in a calm with an opposing swell halting all progress. Eventually the winds returned from the southeast and we passed closehauled between Norta and Diego Islands. Those rocks, rimmed with breaking water and spray, were a grim but beautiful sight.

Three hours later we spotted the Horn – a sight we had sailed halfway round the world to see and one that none of us would easily forget. *Flyer*

Diego Ramirez Islands.

Cape Horn, one of the high
points of the race shared by all
the competitors.

had beaten *Condor* round by twelve miles and it had all been straightfor-
ward sailing: I just couldn't believe our luck. As if the Cape had read my
thoughts, black clouds rolled across to mark another frontal passage. 'More
wind,' I remarked at the time, rubbing my hands with glee; 'that's what we
need to keep pace with *Pen Duick*' – but I didn't reckon on how much.

The first squall to hit was a 50-knot blast, and swinging to a completely
different angle; it caught us with all sail up and the boom lashed down on
the opposite side. It hit with such ferocity that there was no time to think,
and we went into a Chinese gybe. I was letting out the mizzen sheet at the
time and just held on, suspended in mid-air as the yacht lurched over. Rod
was thrown bodily across the deck to land in the scuppers, but everyone
else managed to cling on somehow. For the first time *Flyer* lay trapped,
pinned down by the weight of water in her sails and the wind that blasted in
under the boom. Struggling to get a foothold back on deck, I caught a
glimpse of the mainmast dipping beneath the waves.

Reefing while running
downwind.

Jerry clambered up to release the preventer on the main boom. Aedgard let slip the leeward running backstay, and the sail crashed across smacking the water. The mizzen was also caught, the preventer being jammed in its cleat by the strain on it, so I tore at the halyard and wrenched the sail down. *Flyer* twitched like a boxer out cold. We all wondered if she would be able to beat the count, for water was pouring below through the open hatch. But slowly she stirred, and swinging back up on her feet, unsteadily at first, shook herself down then waited patiently for us to gather our wits.

The 2.2 oz spinnaker was in shreds; the pole had been wrenched from the mast, the slider broken, and sheets washed in all directions. Down below water was everywhere, soaking bedding, sails and clothes. Those off watch who had been having dinner at the time found their food knocked into every corner and ketchup spilt from a smashed bottle was splattered on the cabin ceiling. They retrieved their food and went on eating while we on deck pulled down the remnants of yet another blown spinnaker and re-set the sails. Within ten minutes we had *Flyer* thrusting forward again with a heavy reaching spinnaker set on the spare pole, and within twenty minutes all was ship-shape on deck and we were pumping out.

An hour later we were in big trouble again. Another squall ran up behind, this one at 40 knots, and though we were on the right gybe this time it hit with such force that *Flyer* was driven right through the next wave. The strains on both hull and rig must have been enormous for the nose just buried and carried on down to leave 2 feet of water on deck. That boiling water was like a tidal wave and it tore down the deck prising hands free from their holds and bringing with it bodies, halyards, sheets and anything else that was not well secured. *Flyer* was stopped completely. There was a faint report from above, almost drowned out by the rush of water, and looking up I saw a second spinnaker ripped apart. There was no time to think about consequences. Natural instincts were to fight for air, but eventually *Flyer* staggered out of that watery grave to shake herself down and turn up into the wind. Some people picked themselves out of the scuppers, others had been thrown into the cockpit, but no-one was washed overboard: it was quite incredible that we could survive two near-disasters in less than an hour and come out of at all almost totally unscathed.

The watch was ready to hoist a third spinnaker, but I called out 'Folks, this appears not to be our lucky day for spinnakers – pole out the blast reacher instead.' Once the tattered pieces of spinnaker had been hauled down and the heavy reaching headsail set, we ran for the Strait of le Maire. By this time I had had enough of Cape Horn.

It was just as well, for in this deep cut between mainland and Staten Island, where the bottom plunges down to 176 fathoms within metres of the shore, there was such a steep sea running that we would almost certainly

have lost yet another spinnaker. It was a wild run through the dark, *Flyer* pounding a path through the short waves and carrying a rooster-tail of spray from her stern.

The mountainous 'land of fire' around Cape Horn.

By dawn the last of the snowy peaks were disappearing over the horizon, and the sight of *Condor* five miles astern concentrated our competitive spirit. Our race to stay ahead of her was interrupted by the buzz of a helicopter to herald the arrival of H.M.S. *Endurance*, the British ice patrol ship sent down from the Falkland Islands to watch over the yachts as they rounded the Horn. We talked on the VHF and her radio operator passed over a message from Prince Bernhard, who had been in the area recently. It read 'Best wishes and a safe journey home.' It was a heartening note, and nice to know that the Prince was thinking of us.

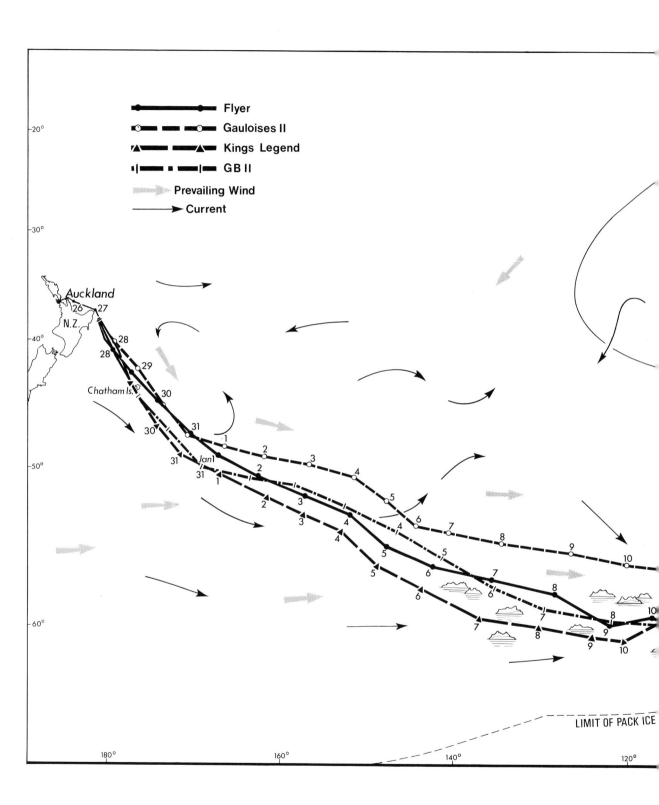

### Legend

- ●━━━━● Flyer
- ○╍╍╍○ Gauloises II
- ◢╍╍╍◢ Kings Legend
- ┃╍·╍┃ GB II
- ▨▨▶ Prevailing Wind
- ───▶ Current

Auckland

N.Z.

Chatham Is.

26  27
28
28
29
30
30
31
31
Jan1
31  1
2
3
4
5
6
7
8
9
10

1
2
3
4
5
6
7
8
9
10

2
3
4
5
6
7
8
9
10

1
2
3
4
5
6
7
8
9
10

-20°
-30°
-40°
-50°
-60°

180°   160°   140°   120°

LIMIT OF PACK ICE

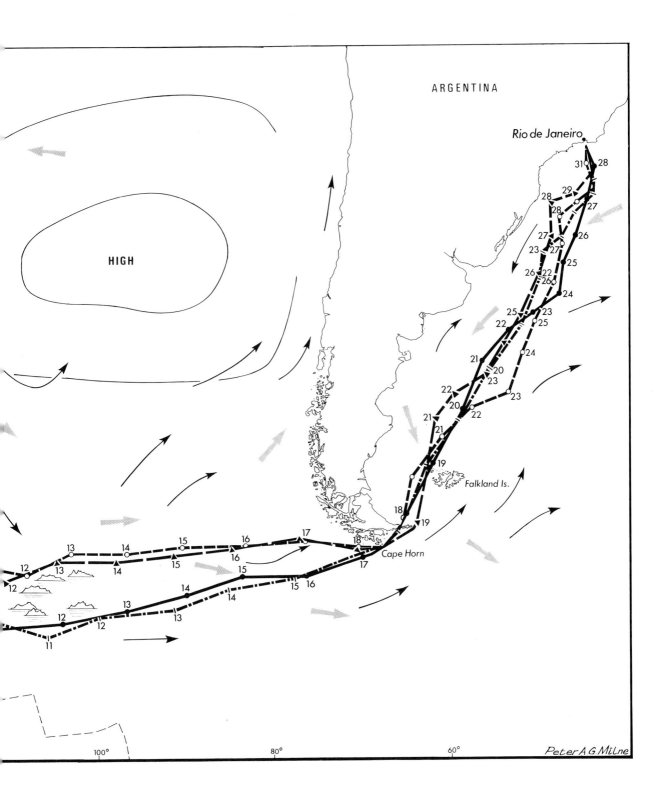

ARGENTINA

Rio de Janeiro

31 28

29
28 27
28
27 26
27 27
23
26 22 25
26
25 23
22 25
24
21 20
22 23
20
21 22 23
21

19
Falkland Is.
18
19

18 Cape Horn
17

HIGH

13 14 15 16 17
12 13 15 16
12 14
12
13 14 15
14 15 16
13
12 13
11

100° 80° 60°

Peter A G Milne

But back to the battle: *Condor* was now abeam and reaching under spinnaker at the same speed as us. After some 4,500 miles without sighting another sail, that close-quarter racing goaded us to get the most out of *Flyer*. *Condor*'s crew tried several sail changes to better their speed, but *Flyer* was on her favourite heading and it soon became apparent that they would need more wind to pass us. It was all great fun, and good to be back in the warmer Atlantic – 'almost like sailing in home waters again', Jerry wrote in the log.

While we enjoyed this close tussle, *GB II* was struck by lightning as she sailed through a violent thunderstorm 300 miles ahead and further to the north. The shock threw Enrique Zulveta from the wheel, and Steve White, furling the mizzen at the time, was knocked onto his back. The mast and rigging glowed under the huge voltage, which also melted the masthead instrument fittings and blew up their electronics. Mysteriously, the radio was not affected, though with the rigging magnetized by the charge navigation became very difficult with unstable compass deviation measuring as much as 70° east. Her crew were extremely lucky, but had to navigate the remaining distance to Rio by sun and star sights alone.

We set a course to the west of the Falkland Islands, hoping for a break in the weather to gain some distance on *Traité de Rome* and *Disque d'Or*. It was the right decision for soon afterwards the weather pattern changed to bring a stiff force 6–7 wind, though it headed us slightly. *Flyer* proved difficult to steer, as irregular, steep short seas continually knocked her off course, but it was fast sailing and the warm spray made a pleasant change from the cold Southern Ocean. We now had more wind than the yachts further south, to give us the advantage in conditions for the first time during this leg. *33 Export* sighted *KL* near the Horn, which gave us her position, so we knew that on January 20, with 1,500 miles left to Rio, *33 Export*, *ADC* and *Kings Legend* were drawing near the Falklands 390 miles astern, while *Condor* lay 30 miles ahead and *GB II* held a further 160 mile advantage over us.

These strong winds continued for another day, but we gybed across in an attempt to gain some easting away from the Brazil current, which at times was running as much as a knot against us. I would have liked to have gained even more ground to the east, to enable us to approach Rio from the south, but the winds were against that; we just had to hope for more favourable conditions later. It proved to be another good day, and while *GB II* and *Condor* pulled further ahead *Flyer* gained considerably on *Traité de Rome*, now 620 miles astern, although *33 Export*, 420 miles astern, was well up with *Gauloises*, probably leading us on handicap for this leg.

The following day, the twenty-ninth since leaving Auckland, saw the winds drop from force 4 to almost nothing. By now Adrian had all the

Spinnaker sheets were rarely cleated during the race and the crew were constantly trimming sail to match the wind.

spinnakers back together again and as the winds faded we changed first from the heavy 2.2 oz to the 1.5 oz, down to the 0.75 oz, and finally finished up with the 0.5 oz floating star to catch the dying breeze.

Apart from H.M.S. *Endurance*, the seas had been totally empty of any shipping so it was a pleasant change to come across the *Senoe*, a Romanian factory fishing vessel, who confirmed our position and gave us the latest weather forecast. Luckily, most of the yachts suffered from calms that day, but at the time we just hoped *Flyer* would not lose too much ground for the Brazil current had pushed us back some 20 miles during the past 24 hours. What we needed was a wind shift to break away.

What came was a northeasterly, and the drifter was replaced with the light genoa. *Flyer* spent the night short-tacking under a brilliant full moon, but while it was fabulous sailing we made very little progress towards Rio. Unfortunately, this northeasterly was not quite the wind shift I have envisaged, and for two days we were badly held back. During the next day the winds built up to 45 knots but remained firmly on the nose, and our distance made good was no more than 120 miles. The only consolation was that from the radio we guessed that the other yachts were doing no better.

Down below, Marcel had his problems too. There had been an unpleasant odour building up in the boat for some time, and lifting up the floorboards to check uncovered the most terrible mess. Jars of peanut

butter, jam, honey and tomato ketchup had all been smashed during the broaching and rolling of the previous days and the sight was enough to make him rush for the companion ladder. It was a gooey, smelly mess, but somehow he managed to clear it all up.

Eventually this storm blew itself out and after a period of calm was replaced by the *pampero limpio* – a local storm that swept up from astern. After our experience at the Horn we kept a keen eye open for any strong squalls, but this time none followed. Instead, we had the unusual experience of sailing with spinnaker straight into head seas. *Flyer* bulldozed her way through, pushing the water aside and casting spray in all directions. It was another fabulous night sail with cloud partially shrouding the full moon to play multicoloured tricks of light on the water. We didn't do so badly either, for despite the unfavourable seas which stopped her almost completely at times, *Flyer* gained handsomely on the yachts ahead. *GB II*'s lead was cut back to 250 miles and *Pen Duick* was plotted 495 miles ahead. But, as was to be expected when we reached this light-weather zone, the boats astern had started to nibble away at our lead, with *Gauloises* now the main threat 393 miles behind. There were no sightings of *Kings Legend* at the time, but we couldn't believe that she would have broken away from the pack without others escaping too, so our overall position on handicap was beginning to look good.

To remind us that the race was far from over yet, the winds suddenly swung back to the north returning the advantage once more to those further south. *Tielsa*, for instance, sailing in far better winds than we had experienced, played the currents around the Falkland Islands to pull herself up to within 272 miles of our position.

Conditions eventually swung back in our favour again and on the thirty-third day produced fabulous sunny weather and a steady force 5 beam wind. *Flyer* was back on her favourite heading once more, sailing at full speed with the now much-repaired 2.2 oz spinnaker set. This wind allowed us to shape a course east of Rio so that we could have some reserve left in hand for the inevitable northeast trades later. *Pen Duick* had now crossed the finish, leaving us with three days in which to cover the last 480 miles and save our time for this leg: we had to average 6.6 knots over the remaining distance, which was quite possible if the winds held.

On January 27, it was Ari's birthday – he was twenty – and to celebrate this and the ever-increasing winds we had beer and wine with our dinner – 'quite a treat for a dry ship.' Another good run left us with 290 miles to go, and 48 hours to beat *Pen Duick*: not impossible. At the time the weather was just incredible, with clear skies, fresh wind and beautifully warm water spraying on deck. During those final hours we gained on most boats except *Condor*, and made up more than 100 miles on *GB II*, who lay becalmed almost within striking distance of the finish.

Further back in the fleet, *33 Export* had problems of a very different nature. Eric Letrosne, a young medical student on board, had been thrown overboard during a violent broach and broke a femur after one leg had been caught in the lifelines. At the time the yacht was 550 miles from Rio and skipper Alain Gabbay, who broke his thumb in the same incident, turned for Rio Grande, the nearest port, some 400 miles away. Though Eric was treated with pain killers, the crew quickly realized that he required urgent hospitalization and immediately radioed for help. The Brazilian Navy first said that a tug would sail out to the yacht from Rio Grande; later the mission was handed to another tug at Florianopolis. In the end no shipping set sail, for this second tug was locked in port by a wrecked tanker although no-one knew this until the following day. *Japy-Hermes*, which had a doctor on board, changed course to meet *33 Export* and offer assistance, but with conditions too rough for their rubber dinghy Doctor Sabarly dived overboard and swam across between the boats. Two days later a reconnaissance aircraft of the Brazilian Air Force guided a helicopter carrying a surgeon towards the yacht as she made for Rio Grande, but Sabarly, judging the transfer to be too dangerous, decided against this rescue and the yacht continued on its course into port, where Letrosne was safely transferred to a hospital.

While this unfortunate chapter was unfolding, we heard on the radio that *GB II* and *Condor* had finished within sight of each other and reckoned they were just twelve hours ahead, if the winds held. The loom of Rio's lights was visible to us 40 miles away, and as *Flyer* drew near the sight was unbelieveable, lights sparkling like stars in the night. Although the winds

Light winds and the mizzen
staysail.

dropped lighter as we neared the coast, they held just long enough for us to finish. Several minutes were wasted in looking for the line; it should have been marked with a red flashing buoy but in fact this was white. We eventually crossed the line at 0323 in good shape with a very happy crew. We had beaten off the challenge from *Kings Legend* and realized then that we had a good chance of winning this leg on handicap.

We had covered 7006 miles over the ground in 34 days, 5 hours, 23 minutes. Eventually *Gauloises II* beat us on handicap by seven hours, having had a final good run to the finish. *Kings Legend* came in two days after us, almost neck and neck with *Disque d'Or* but with a dispirited and demoralized crew. As they came ashore there was defeat in their faces, for this leg had not been a happy one. They finished seventh on handicap for the leg, though retaining second place in the overall race. *Traité de Rome* was third, *Disque d'Or* fourth, and *ADC Accutrac* led the British boats by finishing fifth.

Rio de Janeiro during Carnival Week and the RTWR stopover.

Our stay in Brazil was timed to coincide with the annual Carnival, a week-long festival of processions, colour and high-jinks. It also coincided with the most incredible rain storms to hit Rio for some time, which dampened down much of the enthusiasm. At one time it rained so hard that much of the city was awash, streets transformed into raging torrents. Going to the airport at the time, I was forced to change taxis three times after each became waterlogged under a metre of water. I had never seen rain fall at quite such a rate.

Other problems had their effect on many crews: girls. One could never invite out the local Brazilian ladies without also entertaining an entourage of chaperones, mothers, sisters, aunts and even the odd grandmother or two. It was all very frustrating for those unattached guys who had just spent six or more weeks at sea.

The Yacht Club itself, with its enormous storage facilities and large marina, boasts every convenience and has become a venue for international regattas and races. During our stopover it was preparing for the Soling World Championship, and to my great pleasure I met Geert Bakker again, who is president of the International Soling Association. It is a club that attracts the top levels of Brazilian society, but a year before, members had been left with a very sour taste in their mouths after the visit of some French yachtsmen competing in the Cape-Rio Race. These hallowed premises were subjected to the constant attentions of Copacabana girls boarding Cape Town boats, the playful smashing of crockery, and continual jokes of the sort that required dropped pants for their punchlines. As a club that expects visitors to blend in with the high social standards, was it really any wonder that some Whitbread crews were given a reception cooler than ice? With the memory of that last Cape-Rio Race foremost in their minds, the club had indeed planned for the worst, with the usual guards at the gates and passes issued, not just for entry but for drinking at the bar and swimming in the pool. Problems finally came to a head at the prizegiving where five scantily clad mulatto girls gave Clare Francis the idea to start a samba dance of her own. Within minutes she was joined by 200 or more equally merry guests, who weaved a swerving path through the bar, over chairs and past the astonished hierarchy of Rio, straight into the pool.

The restaurant manager, remembering the obstreperous visitors a year before, rushed to stop the band, but the party continued just the same, others tapping out that infectious beat with whatever was near to hand until all the officials, guests of honour and onlookers had been dragged in to the pool to enjoy the fun. All too soon, though, the party ended. The manager, fearing the worst, called in the riot police, and with tear gas and flailing truncheons they quickly cleared the pool area. It was all very

Adrian thought up this novel way to lessen chafe on lines and sails during the final leg by shrouding the stanchions and lifelines in sailcloth.

unfortunate, but once the Commodore had heard what had happened the manager was sacked on the spot and free compensatory beer appeared on the club balcony.

The next morning I was confronted by a stern-looking Clare Francis who told me that I had thrown her mother in the water. Well, I didn't even know that her mother was there and rushed over to apologise, for it was the least I could do. But far from being coldly chastised for picking on her, I was greeted by this smiling face, and 'Oh Cornelis, it was terrific – I was so worried I might have been left out – you really made my day!' From that moment I knew where Clare got her competitive spirit!

There was a great deal of work to be done on *Flyer* which was now showing signs of wear after three legs and 21,000 miles. Despite our good lead over *Kings Legend* and the rest of the fleet, we had only to suffer one major problem on this final part of the race and that advantage would soon be lost. All suspect rigging was replaced, the foil (removed at Cape Town) refitted to the forestay, and new halyards and sheets put aboard. Bad drinking water had been a matter for complaint since we had left Cape Town, and here at Rio the quality was worse than ever. In fact, it was so bad that Doc thought we might all go down with an epidemic if any was taken on board. There was only one answer, and much to the astonishment of other crews who had set about to try to filter their stocks, a lorry arrived on the quayside next morning to fill our newly scrubbed tanks with bottles of mineral water. It was an expensive solution, but from then on we had no more trouble with the supply – or our stomachs.

Unfortunately, the quality of all food and drink bought in Rio was suspect. The fresh vegetables taken aboard were alive with grubs and of such poor quality that practically all had to be thrown away; half our eggs followed them over the side three days later, when we found they too were bad. Part of the problem with the vegetables was that we were not able to wash them thoroughly before stowing aboard. The jetty where we tied up was open to the bay and subject to a heavy ground swell when the winds came from a certain direction. The motion was so bad that we quickly moved *Flyer* out into the bay, dropping two anchors to hold her. The crew of *Adventure* were not quite so fast and as the swell built up the yacht's bow was badly stove in when it hit the quay. *Flyer*'s anchorage left us with no alternative but to row all the stores out to the boat. This was so time-consuming that it left us with little opportunity to worry about hygiene.

The sails had not arrived from Hood and were apparently lost in transit. Phone call after phone call brought no results, and close to the start I began to get really worried; without those new sails to replace *Flyer*'s then tired and damaged mainsail and no. 1 genoa we would have been left at a severe disadvantage. In desperation, I rang an old neighbour friend now living in Brazil. André Jordan – Mr Fixit – is one of those characters who knows everyone and had got me out of problems before. He went straight to the top, and talking to the Chairman of TWA pointed out that if *Flyer* didn't win this race his airline would then be blamed by the entire Dutch nation for losing her sails. It was made very clear that TWA's nose would be well and truly rubbed in it unless the sails could be found.

This ploy did the trick, for within hours the sails had been traced to another airport and I was promised that they would be on the next plane across. It was all a last-minute rush, but the problems were not completely solved. They still had to clear Customs – a process sometimes taking months that now needed to be achieved overnight. Once again André came to the rescue, and by knowing where to go the right wheels were oiled and the sails handed over just in time for the start of the last leg.

*Flyer* did not commence this last stage of the race as well prepared as I would have liked. Bruce, the engineer in the crew, left the boat to return to Scotland and I took on a young Brazilian, John Anderson, to make up the numbers, who managed quite well considering that he had so little experience of this kind of long-distance racing. There had been few facilities to make repairs at Rio, though some jobs were done by the Brazilian Navy as a favour. Underwater inspection showed some cracks in the filler on the skeg, running parallel to the hull.

This final leg was to be a cat-and-mouse game between *Flyer* and *Kings Legend*. Our task was to cover her and try to retain our $59\frac{1}{2}$ hour overall lead, while Ratcliffe's was to break away and find better winds. I had reckoned his first chance would come as we neared the Doldrums once more, although we realized that the Azores high could also leave us becalmed for a considerable time. If *Flyer* was ever slowed down badly our lead could have been challenged by both *Kings Legend* and *Traité de Rome*, the latter having to make up only 88 hours on handicap. As the fleet left Rio, this race was still very wide open.

# The Calms Threaten

The original plan had been to stage a staggered start from Rio, the slowest yachts leaving first, with the idea that all would arrive back at Portsmouth within a day of each other. This had been done in the first race, but I was very pleased that the Race Committee changed their mind and didn't bend to the wishes of the sponsor. The staggered start can be very unfair because there is always the chance that the fleet would be so split up after the start that individual yachts could well be sailing in completely different weather patterns. Also, the slower ones would have less time for rest and repairs in port.

A small group of spectator boats together with some of the Solings preparing for the World Championship were the sole spectators to this fourth start, on Wednesday, February 22nd. Compared with the grand farewells at Portsmouth, Cape Town and Auckland, their presence put some measure on the degree of interest this race had attracted in Brazil. In fact, we were glad to be away for now the finish was almost in sight.

*Kings Legend* rounded up on us moments before the gun was fired, to cover *Flyer* at the start – I thought. After the trick we had played in Auckland, however, I should have been ready for much worse than mere covering tactics. Much to my surprise they drew alongside not to take our wind but to pelt us with eggs – smelly, rotten, filthy eggs that landed in my face, hair and clothes, and splattered across the deck to draw yellow stains down sails and paintwork. It was one terrible stinking mess and took some time before I saw the funny side of it – unlike *Kings Legend*'s crew, who only broke off the assault once all the 'fresh' eggs had been thrown, killing themselves with laughter.

Starting in light airs and steering a course three miles or so out to sea to keep the sea breeze and wash away the remains of that assault, we quickly gained on the boats further inshore. Indeed, it proved to be a particularly good move, for *Flyer* was the first to round Cabo Frio the next day, while *Pen Duick*, *GB II* and *Condor* fought the fickle winds further inshore.

By the fourth day conditions were no better, holding the yachts in a tight pack. The leaders were continually held up by calms which allowed the

*Flyer* in close to the Sugar Loaf after the start at Rio.

A final look back: the fleet soon after the start of the last leg.

slower ones to catch up. It was all very frustrating, and as we struggled to break clear matters were made even worse when I started to lose champagne on it all. Chris was always one for a bet, and liking a challenge myself we had bottles of champagne staked on almost any point of discussion. How many miles would we run that day? How many miles would the other yachts run? Who would be in the lead? At one point we were sitting becalmed and Chris suggested that the speck on the horizon astern could be *Tielsa*. I just couldn't believe it, for she had never been in sight since we left Portsmouth and was not likely to start sailing faster than *Flyer* now. It was another bottle of champagne lost, for it was *Tielsa* who sailed up within a few hundred metres of us, her spinnaker pulling hard while she enjoyed her own private breeze.

By that night it was obvious that the main body of the fleet was sailing in the same direction as *Flyer*, with the exception of *Kings Legend*. She was sailing a course well inshore and although covering fewer miles than *Flyer* had climbed to the same latitude. Our concern was whether she would pick

up the wind before us. As darkness fell we were treated to the most fantastic thunderstorm, with frightening lightning coming from incredible black clouds to light up the whole sea around us.

Another worry was our freezer. The engine was being run almost continually to freeze our fresh meat, but after five days it was still not cold enough. I wondered if it was a fault with the compressor or merely the warm water outside, now at an even 30°C (86°F), heating up the aluminium hull. There was no way of checking but after eight days' almost continual running the meat was finally frozen hard.

The easterly trade winds eventually filled in on the sixth day and blew a steady force 5; *Flyer* started to make some real headway at last. She does not like to be overpressed when sailing on the wind; 27° is the optimum angle of heel, and if too much sail is set she merely heels further and slows. Optimum performance was always a careful balance between wind and sail, but over the duration of the race we had continued to learn more about exactly which sails to set in the varying wind strengths, and *Flyer* began to fly once more. By that evening *GB II* had pulled furthest ahead with a 70 mile lead and *Pen Duick* and *Condor* fought for two crates of champagne 20 miles astern of her. *Flyer* was fourth, with *Kings Legend*, *Gauloises* and *Traité de Rome* dropping back all the time. From the position reports we then knew that *KL*'s plan to slip ahead along the South American coast had been a failure, which was very reassuring.

Prior to the Clipper Race two years before, Roy Mullender, then skipper of *GB II*, the eventual winner, had done some research on that year's weather pattern in looking for the best spot to break through the Doldrums, and though during the race itself he disregarded this analysis he had benefited greatly by steering a course towards 0°N, 27°W. We intended to take the same route and *Flyer* was followed by most of the other yachts, whose skippers had obviously read the same book. *Kings Legend* was the main exception, persisting with a more westerly course. All we could do was trust in the old adage about safety in numbers and hope that our route was best.

Doc had taken over Bruce's responsibility for the engine on this last leg and had to contend with the deep freeze, and also puzzle over why it was

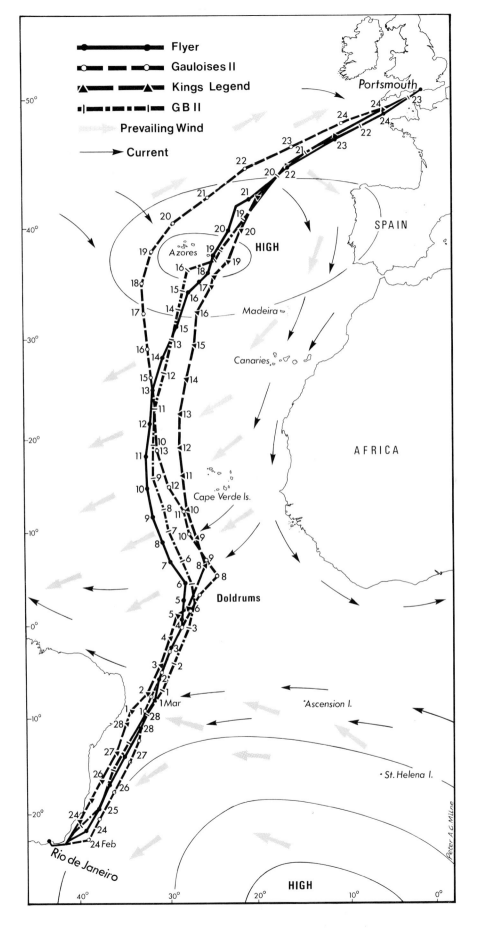

Peter A.G. Milne

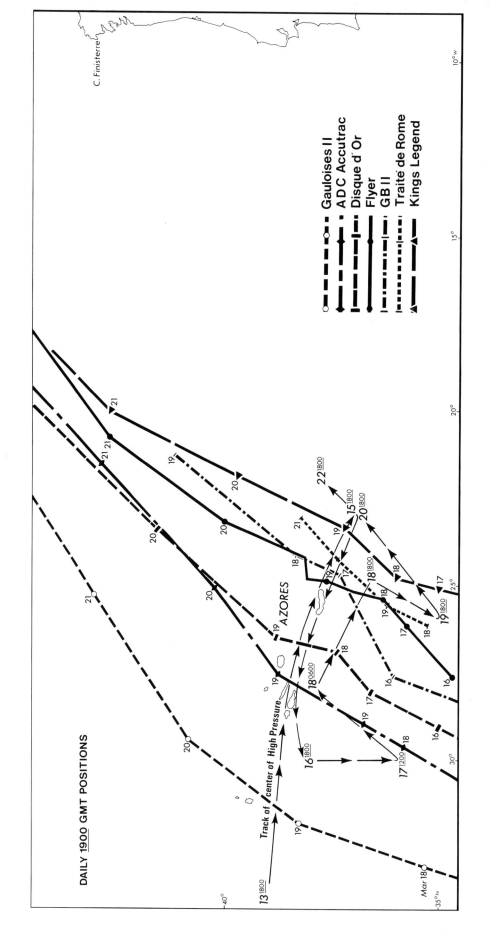

DAILY 1900 GMT POSITIONS

Track of center of High Pressure

AZORES

C. Finisterre

Gauloises II
ADC Accutrac
Disque d'Or
Flyer
GB II
Traité de Rome
Kings Legend

Early-morning celebration on crossing the Equator the second time.

impossible to fully charge the batteries (however, neither expert advice in England nor new batteries ever solved the problem either). In addition a power surge of unknown cause blew out the protection unit for the 'lighting and equipment' alternator, though it served its purpose first, and damaged a couple of instruments. A new spare regulator and surge protection unit were installed and the trouble never occurred again. As well as these mechanical troubles, two of our number were now showing symptoms of a certain post-port syndrome, a result of the pleasures so freely offered back in Rio and a great amusement to the rest of the crew. I had some fun discussing possible treatments over the radio with my good friend Les Williams, now more experienced in these matters, who was also making a head count on *Condor*. Despite their warning in Monrovia, some, it seemed, had gone for a second bite of the cherry.

The weather was now very hot but *Flyer* continued to smash her way through the Atlantic seas towards the Doldrums, making 215 miles in the day. Our position was beginning to look good for with *GB II* just 165 miles ahead, *Kings Legend* 150 miles astern, and *Traité de Rome* a further twelve miles back, we looked like being first on handicap. Somehow the intense heat wasn't quite so bad once Jerry had made that calculation.

*Flyer* crossed the Equator on Saturday, March 4, the eleventh day, 3,690 miles from Portsmouth, and we celebrated with a champagne breakfast. It was another fabulous sailing day but with the winds lightening we decided to set a .75 oz spinnaker and steer off for speed rather than staying closer into the dying breeze under the reacher. This was the same tactic employed to such good effect on the first leg and I just hoped that it would work as well on the return.

We hit the Doldrums in 2°30'N the next morning and the never-ending sail changes began. First we would set the .75 oz spinnaker to cope with the squalls in between calms, then change to the light reacher, windseeker, flanker, drifter, floating starcut and so on, to catch what we could from the changing conditions. We managed to push a further 153 miles in the day but now wind conditions through the Doldrums did not seem as favourable as they had been on the first leg. We had cut through on the same longitude as *Pen Duick* but experienced far more calms. It was very frustrating, for Tabarly reported that he was then 330 miles ahead with a good lead over both *GB II* and *Condor*. Our course had been right: it was the timing that was wrong.

After most of the yachts had passed through this cursed area, by the fourteenth day the positions became clearer. The wind finally returned from roughly northeast to add a further 170 miles to our total but the boats further south were able to gain considerably more easting during their passage through the Doldrums, while we had been pushed westward by the northeast wind. The distances from the various other yachts was approximately the same, but the change in wind direction experienced by those behind us left them well to weather. The next few days were very tense, for if the winds had veered any more *Flyer* would have been in a difficult position.

As we continued to tack into the force 3 headwinds *Kings Legend* became a threat once more. We were 350 miles apart and in completely different winds, and from being 150 miles astern had now drawn level, to bring home the fact that this race was far from over. Where we were there were no signs of the trades whatsoever, and at mid-day *Flyer* lay completely becalmed while the other yachts, both ahead and astern, made gains. It was very worrying, for after being at sea for 15 days, the expected halfway stage, we had covered only 2,454 miles with another 2,946 to go. Again we desperately needed wind, wind and more wind.

It wasn't until the seventeenth day out that we had finally covered half the distance and the trade winds were still far from steady. *Pen Duick* led the fleet 420 miles ahead followed by *GB II* 150 miles behind her. *KL* was at least still on the same latitude as us, though she continued to have a windward advantage. *Traité de Rome*'s radio was malfunctioning, but *Kings Legend* set up a daily schedule with her on the emergency frequency and was thus able to keep track of her, relaying her position daily to the others.

Conditions improved slightly the next day and with winds gusting from force 3 to 6, *Flyer* made a 205 mile run. The flying fish were back with us again, but otherwise there was no sign of life. The fish came aboard in dozens just as they had done on the first leg. However, instead of throwing them all back overboard the port watch placed some of the dead fish into the Dorade box directly above Aegard and Marcel's cabin. They very quickly began to smell in the heat, but it was a full two days before the bad odours were tracked to the ventilation system, for Aedgard was convinced that they came from Marcel's socks!

Eventually the northeasterly winds became more regular in both strength and direction and with the Doldrums now left well behind, tactics were planned to contend with the Azores high, the next stumbling-block on our route back to Portsmouth. The weather reports from Monsanto Radio in Portugal said that this second area of calms was well defined and in its rightful position but would be moving northeast fast. That at least meant we could expect fresh winds for awhile, though *Kings Legend*, now only 50 miles away on the inside of our curve, would also benefit. For nearly three days *Flyer* crashed into head seas without a sail change. Hugh relieved some of the boredom by pulling out his appointment diary for last haircuts before the finish, and Marcel, fed up with cooking, asked if others could

Working on the end of the
boom above the water always
carried a degree of risk.

share some of this chore. It was a sensible idea, for not only did it relieve
some of the boredom but it brought back competitiveness within the crew
with each trying to better the serving before. Meals became something to
really look forward to again and showed what could be done with a little
imagination.

Up on deck, the monotony was only broken when the genoa sheet
suddenly parted, with the metal clew thrashing a wicked path across the
deck as the sail flogged. It was difficult to grasp – one blow on the head
would have knocked a man senseless – but Jerry solved the problem by
passing the lazy sheet round the inner forestay and feeding it back to the
winch.

We were now receiving six-hourly weather reports pinpointing the
position of the high, but its movement was so fast and erratic that it became
impossible to take avoiding action. We could only hold our rhumb line
course and hope to avoid the calms in its midst. *Pen Duick* and *GB II* fell
into this spider's web of calms on the twenty-second day at 34°N, 29°W
and we quickly reduced their lead to within 170 miles as they sat waiting for
wind. However, *Kings Legend* and *Disque d'Or* kept pace with us and were
now leading on handicap. *Traité de Rome* was estimated to be two days

behind along with *Gauloises*, 370 miles astern. From the weather reports the Azores high appeared to be expanding to cover an area 300 miles by 450 miles with the centre of calms moving erratically inside. There seemed to be no way of guessing its path and at the time we just kept fingers crossed that it would keep clear of our course.

Our luck didn't hold out, though. While dolphins, trailing bubbles like wartime torpedoes, tracked our wake, *Flyer* sat almost becalmed. However many sail changes were made there was little we could do to help her, and in the next 24 hours she made no more than 50 miles headway. *Traité de Rome* was reported within 75 miles of our position, *Kings Legend* moved 10 miles ahead, and *Disque d'Or* drew level; for a time *Flyer* seemed the only boat without any wind.

*Condor* went off the air, Robin Knox-Johnston refusing to give his position because she was enjoying a fair breeze well to the west, while we sat and stewed in the hot sun. It made little difference to us – *Condor* was the

Dolphins underneath us in the calm water.

last boat in the handicap standings – but Tabarly and Rob James would have been interested to know for they too lay trapped in the high. However, even without this information it soon became apparent where the winds were, for *Gauloises* made a strong run to the west and sportingly gave this information to the rest of us. Eventually *Flyer* crawled level with the Azores, but it was a very tense time for each minute that ticked away without wind gave *Kings Legend* a better chance to take our lead. When you are becalmed, $59\frac{1}{2}$ hours is a very short time!

On the twenty-sixth day, dawn broke with sunny, warm conditions and a gentle breeze, and with the weather forecast placing the high due south of us at last we had a chance to break clear. We still made very slow progress, just 50 miles that day, but at the time any distance was better than nothing. Every yacht had a better day than we did: *GB II* and *Pen Duick* slipped completely clear of the calms and were now 240 miles ahead going full blast for England. *Gauloises* had pulled right up by steering a more westerly course, *Kings Legend* was still ahead and *Traité de Rome* was reported to be 50 miles astern. We needed wind – and fast.

*Flyer* finally broke out the next day, but not before Aedgard discovered a fractured mast tang holding the starboard runner. We were certainly very lucky (and the routine of daily checks, even in a calm, was justified), for if this had gone un-noticed we might well have lost the mast in the strong

The running backstay tangs in the mast were all but gone five days before the finish and were replaced with steel wire strops around the mast.

winds that followed, and both port and starboard tangs were replaced with temporary wire strops round the mast at the spreaders.

Strong southwesterly winds finally swept through to send us on our way, and with *Kings Legend* just 30 miles ahead and *Traité de Rome* still becalmed astern I now knew that if we held our position to the finish, we would win.

But there were still a few surprises in store. A force 8 gale greeted the leaders as they arrived in the Bay of Biscay, and soon afterwards *GB II* reported a broken boom and two blown-out spinnakers. We lost our 1.5 oz spinnaker in a sudden gust, and later a shackle on a snatchblock holding a reefing pennant to the base of the mast snapped suddenly, to whistle the block past the heads of those in the centre cockpit. We were lucky no-one was hit, but the race was certainly showing a sting in its tail.

As *Flyer* continued towards Portsmouth, the Atlantic swell began to build up to quite enormous heights as we reached at top speed. Indeed, conditions became more reminiscent of the Southern Ocean than anything we had expected in the Western Approaches, forcing us to take down both mizzen and mizzen genoa to lessen the chance of broaching.

*Condor* now came back on the air, Knox-Johnston reporting that they were about to cross the finish line and win the champagne bet from Tabarly. From the same position reports we also heard that *GB II* was 380 miles ahead and *Disque d'Or*, leading us for the first time in the race, had a 110 mile advantage. Our own handicap position for this leg was grim, but from those same position reports I now knew that *Kings Legend* was just 11 miles ahead, almost in sight, and *Traité de Rome* 260 miles astern. We just had to hold on to win.

The westerlies continued to build up to 50 knot gusts, blowing out the No. 2 genoa after it shipped a wave in the foot, and forcing us to take another reef in the main. *Flyer* would probably have gained an extra half knot if we had set the storm spinnaker, but I decided that there was an unwarranted risk of breaking our mast, by overstressing the runner repairs. However, the winds veered further aft soon after, making it safer to hoist the spinnaker, but almost immediately afterwards the port pole was bent 10° after the boat had rolled, dipping the boom into the seas. Chris was also hurt in the incident when the Hi-lift winch handle spun free to give him a nasty crack on the left hand. We were not home and dry by any means yet.

The winds decreased slightly during the evening of March 23, just long enough to allow us to celebrate my birthday with a bottle of champagne over dinner. Then it was back on deck to retrieve the flanker, finally blown out in yet another force 8 squall after surviving 40 knots regularly in the Southern Ocean. There was now 48 hours to go: *Kings Legend* was 20 miles ahead of *Flyer* and fighting to hold her time on *Disque d'Or*, while *GB II*

Changing from no. 1 to no. 2 genoa with too much wind to use the Gemini double-groove headstay for both sails simultaneously.

had just 60 miles left to run for the finish. There was no let-up in the wind and it howled through the rigging to push us on, rolling, surfing, carrying the spray well ahead just as in the Southern Ocean.

The ocean swell decreased rapidly as *Flyer* crossed the 200 metre line on March 23 and came over the continental shelf. But as she turned up into the Channel we were worried about the *Amoco Cadiz* wreck off Brittany. Oil laden spray makes a tremendous mess, staining paintwork, clothes and ruining sails. We had already run through oil slicks way out in the Atlantic, the tell-tale signs that a ship had washed her tanks, and while it was bad enough for us it was disastrous for bird life trapped in the slimy mess.

Running up-Channel in a southwesterly force 6, we made our landfall on St Alban's Head and sighted the Needles, those sharp chalk pinnacles marking the Isle of Wight, and entered the Solent at one in the afternoon on March 25th. There was a small armada of press boats braving what was now a force 8 gale to greet us, and with them were two of my sons. The

*Kings Legend* running home through the Solent an hour ahead of *Flyer* but 59½ hours behind on overall time

Passing the Needles, *Flyer* finds a gale force wind against the tide. The head ring blows out of the weary heavy spinnaker and the sail is gathered in quickly. Within twenty minutes Adrian Ford has it ready for hoisting again, but it is decided to set the shooter instead.

excitement was fantastic: after 5220 miles we now knew *Flyer* had won, and everyone was up on deck. She rolled wildly from gunwale to gunwale; the head ring of the 2.2 oz spinnaker blew out and then the shooter broke free when we took it down, much to the delight of film men and photographers, but with conditions so strong it made little difference to our speed.

After surfing past Cowes at more than 10 knots, we finally rounded up for the finish and crossed closehauled, staying just clear of the Southsea lee shore and heeling nicely in a final 60 knot squall, at 1508 GMT.

We had finished at last – and won.

Ari Steinberg retrieving the halyard after the spinnaker had blown out.

Belting along under poled-out reacher and the shooter, a combination carried in this fashion for the first time during the race.

The tack of the shooter was cut to get it down, and finally everyone is all smiles and relaxing after the troublesome sails have been stowed below and *Flyer* reaches past Cowes.

Just before the finish line the wind rose to 55 knots. The reacher has to be taken down, and with a reefed main and small jib *Flyer* heads for the finish line, too close to the lee shore for comfort.

Conny eating his first green herring for over a year, kindly sent to him by a Rotterdam fish shop.

# Appendices

*FLYER*

## NORMAL GENERAL RULES APPLY FOR THIS SHIP
## SPECIAL REGULATIONS ARE AS FOLLOWS

No smoking below deck.

*Flyer* is a dry ship except for beer.

*Flyer* is a hospitable ship and almost anyone is welcome aboard. Introduction of guests to the Captain is appreciated.

Meals are served according to a pre-arranged menu cycle and should be adhered to by all.

By order of the Captain, the cook can ration certain foods, beverages, water, and other articles.

After using the stove, make certain that the gas supply is turned off.

Light is scarce and always switch off after use.

Switch off the tape recorder after use and replace tape in original box.

Special jobs on board as described in the 'job descriptions' are the responsibility of that particular crew member. Comments or ideas for alterations by anyone are welcome, but should (if possible) be channelled via the responsible crew member.

No personal gear should be lying around the deck or in the cockpits except when drying out.

Watches run from 0–4; 4–8; 8–14; 14–20; 20–24.

Night watches are called 15 minutes before the watch starts and crew members should be on deck on time.

Day watches are called 40 minutes before the watch starts, and meals should be ready 30 minutes before the watch starts.

Cleaning below deck is done by the morning watch.

Cleaning of dishes, etc is done by a member of the 'on watch' crew.

Sail packing is done by the watch who has effected the sail change.

Crew members have assigned bunks. While in harbour, sail bins are used as pipe berths if necessary.

The 'on watch' crew should always remember that the 'off watch' crew is trying to sleep or rest.

The 'off watch' crew can only be called on deck by order of the Captain.

## DESCRIPTION of DUTIES

*Navigator :*

Is part of 'Brainstrust' and standby for port watch.

Is responsible for:

Selection of all charts, pilots, tidal information, etc on board.

Daily determination of the ship's position, either by celestial navigation or dead reckoning.

Having the right weather information at hand.

Handling of the various apparatus marked out for navigation.

VHF radiotelephone

SSB radiotelephone

Recording fathometer

Radio direction finder

Water temperature sensor

Taffrail log

Speedometer

Emergency transmitter

Ship's clocks

Chronometer

Barometer and recording barometer

Sextant

Compasses

Code flags

Recording of the ship's log.

*Cook :*

Is standby for starboard watch.

Is responsible for:

  Galley organization, cooking
  Water distribution

  Liquor and beer distribution (if any)

  Stowage of foodstuffs and recording of daily usage

  Distribution of paper linen

  Keeping below decks clean and tidy.

*Electronicer and Electrician :*

Are responsible for the proper functioning, maintenance, and/or repair of:

*Electric installation*
  Alternators (together with engineer)

  Starting and lighting batteries

  Switchboard

  Shore power system

  Lights and outlets

  Inverter

*Electronic equipment*
  Brookes & Gatehouse equipment

  VHF radiotelephone

  SSB radiotelephone

  Fathometer recorder

  RDF

  All-wave receiver with cassette tape recorder

  Water temperature sensor

  Emergency transmitter

  Locat pocket bleepers

  Hi-fi system, cassette tape deck

Wiring diagram of electrical installation and diagrams and instruction books of all above-mentioned equipment must be on board and are the responsibility of the electrician and electronicer.

*Engineer :*

Is responsible for:

Proper functioning, maintenance and/or repair of the following machines and apparatus on board. Must have adequate knowledge of the equipment to do repairs as needed.

Adequate supply of spare parts, special tools, lubricants, instruction books, etc for the undermentioned equipment:

Volvo diesel engine MD32A with controls in cockpit

Webasto air heater

Various pumps, motor and hand

Alternators (together with electrician)

Cooling unit, deepfreeze, etc

Propeller, shaft, shaft lock and brake bearing

Gas bottles (plus filling)

Exhaust system

Hydraulic backstay adjuster

Hydraulic boom vang

Fire extinguishers.

*Rigger :*

Is responsible for the proper functioning, maintenance and/or repair of:

*Spars*

Mainmast and track

Main boom

Mizzenmast

Mizzen boom (and track)

Shroud rollers

Spinnaker poles

Reaching struts

Spreaders

Mast collars

Standing rigging, blocks, rigging fittings, cleats, turnbuckles, toggles, snatchblocks, blocks. (To maintain maximum performance, check tension readings of shrouds and stays periodically against permanent record.)

Anchors

Cables and docking lines

Fenders

Flag halyards, flagpoles

Lead line

*Safety requirements*

Stanchions, pulpits, lifelines, life rail

Life preservers

Liferafts, including all emergency equipment

Life rings, including overboard safety poles

Radar reflector

*Running rigging* (together with sailmakers and shipwright).


*Sailmaker :*

Is responsible for:

The available sails to be in working condition (and battens).

*Idem* for the running rigging (together with the rigger and shipwright).

Functioning and handling of sewing machine.

Adequate mending material and equipment on board.

*Shipwright :*

Is responsible for the proper functioning, maintenance and/or repair of:

Aluminium on board

Lewmar winches

Steering mechanism (also installing of emergency tiller)

Rudder and rudder stock

Ventilation

Leaks

Water and fuel tanks

Valves and piping, plumbing

Seacocks

Toilets

Washbasins

Woodwork (doors, drawers, lockers, partitions, shelves, etc)

Scuppers

Running rigging (together with sailmaker and rigger)

Treadmaster deck covering

Locks, padlocks

A complete set of tools

Sink anodes

All material and equipment necessary to execute all necessary repairs on items mentioned above, including instructions books, manuals etc.

Knowing the exact places where shores and slings must be placed when beached and hoisted.

*Doctor :*

His task is:

To keep the crew in optimal physical condition.

To give first aid in case of accidents.

To keep the medical kit well stocked after each leg.

To give medical advice (by radio telephone) to other boats in the race.

To see to it that the crew have the right medication while ashore, if necessary.

To know which medical restrictions are in force for the countries we go to and to see that everybody gets the right injections.

## JOBS LIST – AUCKLAND

*Aedgard* assisted by Billy, Chris and Rod
Main boom – either repair or new one.
Handle for hand drill.
Check all mast fittings, swages and bottle screws. New silicon on swage
ends where necessary.
New blocks:
  2 spinnaker masthead (Rondal or Gibb)
  2 running backstays (as present afterguy blocks)
  2 snatchblocks – Gibb.
New spinnaker net out of material without chafing qualities.
Check safety provisions.
Hydraulics – Yachtspars.
Fix spinnaker halyards outside mast as an alternative and two new
blocks on deck before the mast.
Enlarge spinnaker halyard exits.
New sleeves on spinnaker pole and main boom.

*Gerard*
Check charts, pilots, etc for next leg and buy as necessary.
Check crystals for Sirius radio.
Check compasses, repair and compensate.
Bring various blocks from Holland.
Plotting, weather recording paper, etc.

*Hugh* assisted by Chris
Forward hatch.
Repair/replace afterguy eyes on toerail.
Steering wheel, provision to be made so that shaft running into pedestal
cannot slip out.
Steering cable – 1 spare galvanized.
Service Lewmar winches.
Stanchions and base plates.

Replace base plate for lifeline aft.
Repair plastic toerail cover.
2 jockey poles on deck. Get brackets made (check with Aedgard).

*Bruce*
Engine: get local Volvo dealer for repairs and service.
Alternators to be serviced.
New belts.
Check and repair deepfreeze.
Check fuel oil.
Check Webasto heater.
Repair dustbin.

*Adrian* to be assisted by Billy, Bruce, Rod and Hugh
Check construction and delivery of new sails:
  1 × 2.2 oz spinnaker
  1 × 1.5 oz spinnaker
  1 × 2.6 oz flanker
  1 × 2.6 oz shooter
  1 × 1.5 oz mizzen spinnaker
  1 × 2.2 oz head patch.
Check rebuilding/repair of:
  1.5 oz spinnaker
  Heavy genoa no. 1
  Chafe patches genoas nos. 2 and 3
  Mizzen staysail
  Mizzen spinnaker .75 oz
  2.2 oz spinnaker head patch
  Leech of no. 1 mizzen
  Leech lines in main as discussed with Jerry.
Check all sails we used last leg and repair where necessary.
Rotate steering wheel.
We stay with hanks for Leg 3.
Leather patches on forward stanchions.
Sort out sail battens.
New shroud covers where necessary (Dacron?).

*Ari*
Masthead navigation light.
Electrical wiring and connections to compasses.
Electrical wiring and connections to navigation lights.
Fix light in clock dodger.
Check torches, and advise on possible new ones.

Assist others where possible.
Check B & G gear, specially wind meters (360°, closehauled, and speed) with local B & G man.

*Marcel*
Buy 4 new plastic water containers.
Prepare list of necessary food and beverages for third leg.
Advise on new galley utensils.
Collect Mountain House food and check contents.
Water in water tanks.
Aedgard oversees stowage.
Keep ship clean below deck, including head, during Auckland stay.

*Bert*
Check and replenish medical supplies.
Keep deck clean daily with water during Auckland stay.
*NOTE :* WITHOUT MY PERMISSION IT IS NOT ALLOWED TO LEND ANYBODY TOOLS OR MATERIALS BELONGING TO *FLYER*.

## SAIL LIST

| Sail | Area m² | Weight U.S. oz |
|---|---|---|
| Windseeker (2) | 100 | 0.75/1.5 |
| Drifter | 122 | 2.2 |
| Light H1 genoa | 122 | 4.1 |
| Heavy H1 genoa (2) | 121 | 8.2 |
| H2 genoa | 103 | 8.2 |
| H3 genoa | 83 | 10.5 |
| Light reacher | 122 | 4.1 |
| Blast reacher | 94 | 8.2 |
| Large jib | 58 | 8.2 |
| Small jib | 28 | 10.5 |
| Big boy (Staysail) (with reef) | 76 | 4.1 |
| Genoa staysail | 60 | 4.1 |
| Forestaysail | 31 | 8.2 |
| Tallboy (hardly used) | 35 | 2.2 |
| Mizzen spinnaker | 70 | 1.5 |
| Mizzen staysail (2) | 70 | 1.5 |
| Mizzen genoa | 50 | 4.1 |
| Floating star | 291 | 0.5 |
| Floater (2) | 291 | 0.5 |
| Light spinnaker (2) | 291 | 0.75 |
| Medium spinnaker (2) | 291 | 1.5 |
| Heavy spinnaker (2) | 291 | 2.2 |
| Super flanker (2) | 240 | 2.6/2.2 |
| Storm spinnaker (only used once) | 150 | 2.7 |
| Small storm spinnaker (discarded) | 70 | |
| Shooters | 123 | 1.5 light 2.2 heavy |
| Storm staysail (not used) | 16 | 10.5 |
| Trysail (not used) | 17 | 10.5 |

| *Apparent wind speed* | *Apparent angle* | *Bag code stripes* |
|---|---|---|
| 0–5 kts | 25°–120° | Red top, no stripes |
| 4–7 | 25°–90° | One 1″ green |
| 6–16 | 25°–50° | One 3″ green |
| 14–25 | 25°–45° | One broad green |
| 23–30 | 25°–45° | Two green |
| 30–40 | 25°–50° | Three green |
| 6–25 | 50°–100° | One red |
| 20–40 | 50°–140° | One broad red |
| 35–45 | 30°–150° | Green bag, one yellow |
| 35–55 | 30°–180° | Green bag, two yellow |
| 8–25 | 70°–120° | Red top, one black |
| 8–30 | 50°–120° | Red top, two black |
| 20–30 | 30°–180° | Red top, three black |
| 10–35 | 160°–180° | One blue |
| 8–25 | 120°–180° | Red bag, one black |
| 4–25 | 90°–150° | Red bag, two black |
| 8–30 | 60°–120° | Red bag, three black |
| 3–7 | 45°– 70° | |
| 3–7 | 60°–180° | No stripes – 0·5 oz |
| 6–12 | 60°–180° | One blue – 0.75 oz |
| 10–20 | 60°–180° | Two blue – 1.5 oz |
| 18–35 | 90°–180° | Three blue – 2.2 oz |
| 10–40 | 60°–180° | One broad blue FL |
| 40–50 | 120°–180° | Two broad blue ST |
| 50 | 120°–180° | |
| 10–35 | 130°–180° | Yellow top, one yellow |
| 50+ | 35°–180° | White bag |
| 50+ | 35°–180° | White bag |

## 'BEER HANDICAP'

| | |
|---|---|
| *ADC Accutrac* | 20 cases |
| *Adventure* | 6 |
| *B & B Italia* | 12 |
| *Heath's Condor* | 75 |
| *Debenhams* | 16 |
| *Gauloises II* | 20 |
| *Kings Legend* | 40 |
| *Japy-Hermes* | 10 |
| *Tielsa* | 20 |
| *Traité de Rome* | 40 |
| *Disque d'Or* | 10 |
| *Great Britain II* | 20 |
| *Neptune* | 10 |
| *Flyer* | 0 |

Whitbreads arranged for each boat to be supplied with whatever amount of complimentary beer they required. The above list is the 'beer count' handicapping table.